WELCOME TO MY KITCHEN

Joan McElman

MACINTYRE PURCELL PUBLISHING INC.

Copyright 2016 MacIntyre Purcell Publishing Inc.

All rights reserved. No part of this book covered by the copyrights hereon may be reproduced or used in any form or by any means – graphic, electronic, or mechanical – without the prior written permission of the publisher. Any request for photocopying, recording, taping, or information storage and retrieval systems of any part of this book shall be directed in writing to the Canadian Reprography Collective, 379 Adelaide Street, West, Suite M1, Toronto, Ontario, M5V 1S5.

MacIntyre Purcell Publishing Inc.
194 Hospital Rd.
Lunenburg, Nova Scotia
B0J 2C0
(902) 640-3350

www.macintyrepurcell.com
info@macintyrepurcell.com

Printed and bound in Canada by Marquis

Design and layout: Channel Communications and Alex Hickey

Photo Credits:
Michelle Ricketts: pages 7, 9, 11, 15, 17, 18, 21, 23, 25, 28, 31, 32, 46, 50, 56, 58, 64, 66, 76, 79, 64, 81, 82, 87, 88, 91, 93, 106, 117, 125, 139, 146, 161, 165 Taylor Cameron: pages 36, 39, 43, 53, 54, 62, 70, 73, 110, 149, 158, 164, 169

Library and Archives Canada Cataloguing in Publication

McElman, Joan, author   Welcome to my kitchen / Joan McElman.

ISBN 978-1-927097-90-8 (paperback)

1. Cooking. 2. Cookbooks. I. Title.

TX714.M3345 2016   641.5   C2016-902196-3

MacIntyre Purcell Publishing Inc. would like to acknowledge the financial support of the Government of Canada and the Nova Scotia Department of Tourism, Culture and Heritage.

Dedication

I would like to dedicate this book to my wonderful sister-in-law Karin, who was as close to me as a mother. Without her and Bill, my brother, I'd have never made it out of my teenage years. For all the love and support you offered, I salute you. Rest in peace and thank you for all you did for me and for raising such wonderful nieces, who are like sisters to me.

Foreword

First impressions mean a lot and I remember well my first meeting with Joan McElman. I had recently joined Eastlink TV and wanted to watch a taping of one of the channel's better known programs, *Welcome to My Kitchen* and meet its star. Arriving on the set, I gained a wonderful, lasting impression of Joan.

The program was being taped in a converted cable office that had seen better days – it had been a challenge to make this into a TV studio. It was reminiscent of the early, pioneer days of community TV. The technologically rustic environment did not deter Joan – or our production team.

Joan zipped around the small space undaunted by the many obstacles in her way. Working with a layout that included a microwave lodged in a former payment window opening, Joan prepared a full course meal. She provided cooking tips – a takeaway for me was to salt pasta cooking water – and produced a superb meal (devoured in minutes by our crew once taping ended – a common ritual and the secret to easily sourcing a crew to work on Joan's program).

When people talk about TV personalities being true professionals, they mean people like Joan. As long-time host of *Welcome to My Kitchen*, Joan produces a weekly program in which she researches the recipes (hundreds so far), tests the dishes, cooks the meals (sometimes pre-cooking ingredients at her home and bringing them to the set) and appears on air – by herself – all in a volunteer capacity. Amazing!

The program *Welcome to My Kitchen* has remained a top-viewed program on Eastlink TV for many years. Generations of Maritimers have learned cooking skills and recipes from Joan McElman.

Michael Smith
Vice President, Eastlink TV

Introduction

I was brought up on a farm and we grew pretty much all of our own food. The youngest of a large family, I was in the kitchen with my mother a lot. I learned to cook from scratch at a very early age. When I got married, I could cook but only very basic recipes: roast beef, stew, homemade soups and lots of desserts.

My husband was in the military and we moved fairly often. We were exposed to different communities and ethnic groups every time my husband was posted to a new base. Wherever we were sent, I enjoyed being part of the dynamic and diverse military base life. Along with the local culture, at each posting there was always a fairly extensive group of exchange officers – from the U.S., the U.K., Australia, the Netherlands, etc. – adding to the mix.

As our lives evolved, my husband had opportunities to travel to various other lands. Everywhere he went, when he tasted something he liked he would ask for the recipe and bring it home to me. Our palates changed to include many different cuisines and cultures. As we put this book together, it's been a real treat to review things we tried years ago and be reminded of our connection to all the communities we have lived in.

I would like to acknowledge Eastlink TV for all the help in compiling this book. I would also like to thank my husband for all his help and encouragement. I especially acknowledge the inspiration from my late sister-in-law, Karin, who taught me so much about cooking and whose knack for creating a wonderful meal from virtually nothing really sparked my enthusiasm for the kitchen.

I am so pleased to say that both my children and their spouses share my love for cooking and creating good food. I hope they will pass it on to their children as well.

The greatest compliment I've ever received from fans was that through *Welcome to My Kitchen* I had taught them how to cook.

I hope our fans will continue to watch the show for the new recipes we will be developing in the future.

Joan McElman

BREADS AND GRAINS

I love having muffins on hand – I usually make a dozen or so, freeze them and then you can put them in the microwave for 15 to 20 seconds and have hot, fresh muffins. Only muffins with no fat content cannot be reheated – they get very tough.

Rhubarb Muffins

½ cup sour cream or yogurt
¼ cup oil
1 large egg
1⅓ cups flour

1 cup diced rhubarb
⅔ cup brown sugar
½ tsp baking soda
¼ tsp salt

TOPPING

¼ cup brown sugar
¼ cup chopped pecans or walnuts

½ tsp cinnamon
2 tsp melted butter

Combine ingredients. Fill greased or paper-lined muffin cups ⅔ full. Sprinkle topping over.

Bake 25 to 30 minutes at 350°F.

Another time, we were staying in New Brunswick at our cottage and had travelled to Fredericton to the market. A lady approached me and said she was a fan. I introduced my husband, my brother-in-law and my sister-in-law to her and we left. My sister-in-law asked who that was. I had to tell her that I had no idea.

Maple Apple Muffins

1¼ cup oatmeal
½ cup maple syrup
1½ cups milk
1 egg
2 cups flour
¼ cups butter

1 tbsp baking powder
1 tsp vanilla
½ tsp salt
2 cups finely diced peeled apple
⅓ cup sugar
2 tbsp maple syrup (for topping)

Heat oven to 400°F. Combine oatmeal, maple syrup and milk. Let stand 10 minutes. Combine dry ingredients, whisk in sugar, egg, butter and vanilla. Stir in oatmeal mix. Pour into greased muffin pans. Bake 25 minutes or until cooked through. Let cool 10 minutes, then brush tops with maple syrup. Cool on rack.

Super Blueberry Muffins

This recipe is amazingly good, however, if you intend to freeze them, do not put the lemon sugar topping on as it turns syrupy in the freezer. I usually freeze them plain, then put the sugar topping on when I thaw them.

2 cups flour
½ cup sugar
3 tsp baking powder
Dash of salt
Rind of 1 lemon

1 egg
1 cup milk
⅓ cup melted butter
1 cup blueberries

Mix dry ingredients. Mix wet ingredients and combine just until moistened. Fold in blueberries. Bake in muffin cups (sprayed with cooking spray or lined with paper) for 20 minutes at 400°F. Let stand 5 minutes. Remove from pan.

TOPPING
¼ cup melted butter
1 tbsp lemon juice
Sugar (spread on clean work surface or plate)

Combine butter and lemon juice. Dip top of each muffin in this mixture, then roll in sugar.

Apple Oat Muffins

¾ cup oatmeal
2 cups flour
¾ cup yogurt or sour cream
¾ cup brown sugar
2 eggs
4 tsp baking powder
1 cup shredded apple

2 tsp cinnamon
¼ cup oil
1 tsp baking soda
1 tsp vanilla
½ tsp nutmeg
½ tsp salt
½ cup raisins

Soak oatmeal in yogurt for 10 minutes Whisk in remaining wet ingredients. Mix dry ingredients together in a large bowl. Gently combine and mix only until moistened. Fold in apple. Spoon batter into greased or paper-lined muffin cups and bake at 375°F for 20 to 25 minutes

One of the things I've learned over the years is how to substitute for ingredients that are not readily available in your area. For example, one can substitute green beans (whole) for snow peas if the latter aren't available. I have often substituted a tablespoon of lemon juice in milk for buttermilk. Works fine. If you are short of eggs, you can add an additional tablespoon of vegetable oil for each egg. You still need some egg, but it will work.

Honey Oat Bran Muffins

½ cup natural bran
¾ cup liquid honey
1 cup oatmeal
2 eggs, beaten
¾ cup wheat germ
½ cup oil
1 tsp cinnamon

1 cup flour
½ tsp salt
2 tsp baking powder
1 cup sour milk or buttermilk
1 tsp baking soda
½ cup raisins

Combine bran, oats, wheat germ, cinnamon and salt. Add milk and let stand 30 minutes. Add honey, eggs and oil, mix well. Add flour, baking powder and soda all at once. Stir until just moistened. Bake in prepared muffin tins for 20 to 25 minutes at 375°F.

Pina Colada Muffins

½ cup sugar
1 egg
¼ cup butter
1 cup yogurt or sour cream
1 tsp vanilla
1½ cups flour

1 tsp baking powder
½ tsp baking soda
½ tsp salt
¾ cup crushed pineapple, well drained
½ cup coconut

Mix first 5 ingredients together to blend. Add dry ingredients only until moistened. Add pineapple and coconut. Pour into prepared muffin tin and bake at 350°F for 20 to 25 minutes.

Overnight Cinnamon Rolls

20 frozen bread rolls
1 cup brown sugar
¼ cup instant vanilla pudding
2 tbsp cinnamon
¾ cup raisins
½ cup melted butter

Grease a 10-inch bundt pan. Place frozen rolls in pan. Mix sugar, pudding mix, cinnamon and raisins. Sprinkle over rolls. Pour melted butter over all. Cover with a clean, dry cloth. Leave on counter overnight. When you are ready to bake the rolls, preheat oven to 350°F. Bake for 25 minutes. Let stand 5 minutes. Turn out onto serving plate.

One day, long before I had customized aprons, we were doing the cooking show in Aylesford and my director said, "Joan, you'd better start wearing an apron. You keep dipping your left breast in the flour." Sure enough, there were white smudges on my top. After that, I always wore an apron.

Cranberry Cheese Bread

1¼ cups cranberries
¼ cup sugar
2 cups flour
¾ cup sugar
½ tsp baking soda
1½ tsp baking powder
½ tsp salt
Juice of one orange
2 tbsp melted butter
1 egg, beaten
2 tsp grated orange rind
1½ cup shredded cheese
½ cup chopped walnuts (optional)

Rinse and halve cranberries. Mix cranberries with ¼ cup sugar. Combine dry ingredients and set aside. Mix orange juice with enough water to make ¾ cup. Add orange rind. Beat together with butter, egg and cheese. Stir in dry ingredients. Add cranberries and nuts. Bake in a floured and oiled (sprayed with cooking spray) loaf pan at 350°F for about 1 hour.

Molasses Oat Bread

1 cup whole wheat flour
1¼ cups all purpose four
1 tsp salt
1 tbsp baking powder
1 tsp baking soda
1½ cups buttermilk
1 egg
2 tbsp oil
1 tsp vanilla
½ cup chopped walnuts
½ cup molasses
1 cup oatmeal

Mix dry ingredients, except oatmeal and set aside. Mix wet ingredients and oatmeal; let stand 10 minutes. Add dry ingredients. Pour into a greased loaf pan and bake at 350°F for about an hour or until toothpick inserted in centre comes out clean.

Cranberry Scones

2 cups flour
10 tsp sugar, divided
1 tbsp grated orange zest
2 tsp baking powder
½ tsp salt
⅓ cup butter, cold
1 cup dried cranberries
¼ cup yogurt
1 tsp baking soda
¼ cup orange juice
1 egg
1 tbsp milk

Combine flour, 7 teaspoons of sugar, orange zest, baking powder and salt in food processor bowl. Add butter, 1 tablespoon at a time, until coarse crumbs form. Transfer this mixture to mixing bowl. Add baking soda to yogurt; stir until frothing stops. Add orange juice and milk. Blend together just until moistened. Turn out onto floured surface. Knead 6 to 8 times. Pat into an 8-inch circle. Cut into 10 wedges. Brush with milk, sprinkle with remaining sugar. Bake 12 to 15 minutes at 400°F.

Raisin Nutmeg Muffins

This is one of the recipes that does not freeze well as there is very little fat in them. But they are diet friendly.

2 cups flour	1 lemon
½ cup sugar	1 cup skim milk
2 tsp baking powder	2 tbsp oil
½ tsp nutmeg	⅔ cup raisins
½ tsp salt	

Combine dry ingredients. Grate 1 teaspoon zest from lemon into bowl; add egg, milk and oil. Add the raisins, then stir in dry ingredients. Spoon batter into prepared muffin tins. Bake at 400°F for 15 to 20 minutes.

When my granddaughter was going to Mount Allison University, she and her friends would frequently tune in to the cooking show (apparently, there was some sort of drinking game involved.) She would loudly declare, "That's my grandma", but no one would believe her. We look nothing alike. After she told me this, I took care to announce during an episode of the show that Anna was indeed my granddaughter. When she came to Acadia University closer to my home to do her second degree, she made everyone there aware exactly who her grandmother was.

Oatmeal Orange Muffins

1 cup oatmeal	1 cup raisins
1 cup orange juice	1 cup flour
½ cup butter	1 tsp baking powder
½ cup sugar	1 tsp baking soda
½ cup brown sugar	1 tsp salt
2 eggs	1 tsp vanilla

Combine oatmeal and orange juice in small bowl; let stand 10 minutes. In a large bowl, cream together butter and sugars. Beat in eggs; then add oat mixture. Add dry ingredients, raisins and vanilla. Pour into prepared muffin cups. Bake 20 minutes at 375°F.

Apple Cranberry Muffins

This recipe is the only one where you can put the topping on to bake and then freeze them. It doesn't come apart when reheating.

2¼ cups flour
1½ cups brown sugar
1 tsp baking soda
1 egg

1 cup yogurt
½ cup oil
2 chopped apples
¾ cup cranberries, chopped

TOPPING
¼ cup brown sugar
¼ cup chopped slivered
   almonds, toasted

3 tbsp oatmeal
½ tsp cinnamon
1 tbsp butter, melted

Combine egg, yogurt and oil. Add dry ingredients. Mix only until moistened. Fold in apples and cranberries. Pour into prepared muffin tins. Sprinkle with topping. Bake at 375°F for about 25 minutes.

Banana Muffins

1½ cups sugar	½ tsp salt
3 eggs	1 tsp cinnamon
¾ cup oil	1 tsp allspice
2 cups flour	2 cups mashed bananas
2 tsp baking soda	½ cup raisins (optional)

Preheat oven to 350°F. Beat sugar and eggs until creamy; beat in oil. Add dry ingredients. Mix in bananas and raisins. Pour into prepared muffin cups and bake 20 minutes or until toothpick inserted in centre comes out clean.

I usually have one or two leftover bananas, so I freeze them in their peel, in freezer bags, until I have enough to make muffins. When I thaw them, I place them in a strainer and let the liquid drip out so the muffins won't be soggy.

Toffee Loaf

1¼ cups (300 ml) sweetened condensed milk	1 cup water
	1 cup butter

Bring to boil and simmer 3 minutes, stirring constantly.

Add:

1 cup raisins	1 cup chopped dates
¾ cup currants	

Let cool.

2 cups flour	⅛ tsp salt
1 tsp baking soda	

Combine flour, baking soda and salt and add to the wet ingredients.

Pour batter into a greased loaf pan. Bake at 350°F for 1¾ hours, until toothpick inserted in centre comes out clean.

APPETIZERS

Back in the day when we were young and stupid, we used to host cocktail parties and were always on the lookout for good, make-ahead recipes that we could serve with drinks. Now that we're older and wiser, these make really good appetizers or snacks while playing cards, etc.

Layered Crab Dip

8 oz cream cheese, softened
1 tbsp finely grated onion
1 tbsp Worchestershire sauce
2 tsp lemon juice
½ cup seafood cocktail sauce
7 oz crabmeat, drained and picked over to make sure there is no shell left
2 tbsp chopped parsley

Mix cheese, onion, Worchestershire sauce and lemon juice together. Spread on a shallow serving dish. Spread cocktail sauce over, leaving a ½-inch border of cheese. Spread drained crab over. Sprinkle with parsley and serve with assorted crackers.

Hot Mushroom Turnovers

These are among my favourites but they are fussy to make. I usually use the food processor to chop the mushrooms, as this makes them nice and fine, which makes for a much better texture.

PASTRY

1 (8 oz) (250 g) pkg cream cheese   1½ cups flour
½ cup butter

Combine cream cheese and butter, add flour. Shape into a ball. Cover with plastic wrap and refrigerate at least 1 hour.

FILLING

¼ lb (113 g) mushrooms, finely chopped (Use a food processor to chop, if possible)
1½ tbsp butter
2 tbsp sour cream
1 tbsp flour
½ tsp salt
⅛ tsp thyme

Sauté mushrooms in butter, cook until liquid has evaporated. Remove from heat, add remaining ingredients. Roll pastry out to ⅛ inch. Cut with round 3-inch cookie cutter, placing half a teaspoon of mushroom mixture in centre of circle. Brush edges with beaten egg, fold over and crimp edges. Prick tops. Place 1 inch apart on ungreased baking sheets. Bake 12 minutes at 450°F. These may also be made into mini-tarts, but decrease baking time to about 10 minutes.

Putting this book together has been an interesting trip down memory lane. I've fondly recalled all the wonderful ladies who contributed to my knowledge and gave me access to recipes. Our military ladies' club always hosted an International Dinner. Each exchange wife would bring dishes representing the country she came from. We always traded recipes — it was an important part of our bond as friends. Some of those women are in touch with me to this day. I'm especially appreciative of a particular Canadian lady who was married to an Aussie — she and I became really good friends. It was amazing the recipes she supplied me with! When she returned to Australia, she found the time and goodness of heart to send me a set of Australian Women's Weekly cookbooks. They have been such a great resource. Not all of the ingredients are available here in Canada, but it's been fun trying to find things to replace them.

Party Bread Fondue Pot

1 loaf unsliced, firm bread (sourdough, preferably)
1 (8 oz) (250 g) pkg cream cheese
1 cup sour cream
1 cup grated cheese
½ cup mayonnaise
2 oz (56 g) smoked ham, finely chopped
¼ cup sliced green onions
1 tsp Worcestershire sauce
½ cup chopped green chilies

Cut the top off the loaf of bread. Hollow out the interior like a jack-o-lantern, leaving a ½-inch crust all the way around and reserving the pieces of bread from the inside. Tear bread removed from the inside of the loaf into chunks for dipping and place pieces in a plastic bag to keep them from drying out. Mix all other ingredients and pour into hollowed-out bread bowl; set the top of loaf in place. Wrap in double thickness of tin foil and bake at 350°F for about 1 hour, until the filling is hot all the way through. Serve with the bread bits on the side, along with crackers. When the chunks run out, you can tear the bowl apart and eat it, too.

Cheese and Broccoli Fondue

¼ cup butter
½ cup chopped onion
½ cup chopped celery
1 cup sliced mushrooms
2 (10 oz) (285 g) pkgs chopped broccoli or spinach, rinsed and drained
8 oz processed cheese, cubed
1 clove garlic, chopped
2 (284 ml) cans cream of mushroom soup
½ cup chopped pecans
¼ cup sherry, sauterne, or any white wine

In a saucepan, sauté onion, celery and mushrooms in butter. Add broccoli and heat on low until warm; add remaining ingredients. Place in a greased casserole or a small slow cooker. Bake at 325°F for 45 minutes, or in slow cooker at low heat for 2 to 3 hours. Place in serving dish and serve with corn chips.

Spinach Dip

2 (10 oz) (285 g) packages frozen chopped spinach (thawed)
4 green onions, sliced
1 envelope dry vegetable soup mix
1 cup mayonnaise
2 cups sour cream
1 (6 oz) (295 ml) can water chestnuts, chopped

Drain the spinach well and squeeze dry. Mix remaining ingredients and let stand for 2 hours (to rehydrate the dried vegetables). Serve with vegetables or crackers. Alternatively, you can take a round loaf of pumpernickel bread, cut the top off, hollow the loaf out, put the dip into it and serve with the bread chunks.

Chicken Bombs

2 chicken breasts, diced
3 jalapeno peppers, seeded and cubed
12 slices bacon
BBQ sauce

Lay ½ slice of bacon on work surface. Top with 1 piece of chicken, 1 slice jalapeno, another piece of chicken and wrap bacon slice around. Secure with a toothpick. Brush with BBQ sauce. Bake at 400°F for 20 to 25 minutes until bacon is crisp. This works really well on the BBQ.

Veggie Pizza

2 pkgs unbaked crescent roll dough
2 (8 oz) (250 g) pkgs cream cheese
¾ cup mayonnaise
1 envelope ranch dressing mix
Assorted chopped vegetables, e.g. tomatoes, cauliflower, broccoli, green peppers, mushrooms, green onions
¾ cup chopped black olives
1 cup shredded cheddar cheese

Spread crescent rolls out flat in a jelly roll pan. Bake 12 to 15 minutes at 400°F, until brown. Let cool completely. Cream together the cream cheese, mayonnaise and dressing mix. Spread over crescent roll crust. Sprinkle the vegetables over the cream cheese mixture and press down so they stick. Sprinkle with cheddar cheese and chopped olives. Chill 2 hours.

Camembert Roll

This recipe came to me from an Australian exchange wife and is great because it must be made well ahead of time. It doesn't hurt it to be rewrapped and pulled out again at another time – if you ever have leftovers.

5 oz (150 g) Camembert
½ cup cheddar cheese, grated
2 tbsp mayonnaise
2 tsp Dijon mustard
6 green onions
Pepper
½ cup (125 g) smoked almonds, finely chopped

Remove rind from camembert. Put all ingredients, except almonds, in food processor (or beat with mixer) and process until well combined. Form into log shape. Roll in finely chopped almonds. Wrap in foil or plastic wrap. Chill well. Serve with crackers.

Smoked Salmon and Mozzarella

This recipe is also one that came from my Australian friend, Rosemary – she is an amazing cook and we remain friends to this day.

8 slices bread
½ cup butter
½ tsp Dijon mustard
1 clove garlic, minced
2 tsp capers, chopped
1 tbsp chopped parsley
4 slices mozzarella
4 slices smoked salmon

Cut 2-inch circles or squares in bread. Melt half the butter. Brush both sides of bread with melted butter and bake 10 minutes at 350°F, until golden. Remove and cool. Beat remaining butter with garlic, Dijon, chopped parsley and chopped capers. Spread over one side of bread. Cut salmon to fit bread slices. Place salmon on bread, top with equal size slice of mozzarella. Bake 10 minutes at 350°F until melted.

Spinach Cheese Triangles

⅓ cup finely chopped onion
1 tbsp butter
1 (10 oz) (285 g) pkg frozen spinach, thawed and squeezed dry
1 cup grated parmesan
¾ cup shredded mozzarella
2 tbsp crumbled feta

2 eggs, beaten
2 tbsp breadcrumbs
¼ tsp salt
Pepper
12 sheets phyllo pastry, thawed
Butter-flavoured cooking spray

Melt butter in a deep frying pan. Add onion and sauté until tender. Stir in spinach and cook until all liquid is evaporated. Add to bowl with cheeses, crumbs, salt and pepper. Place one sheet of phyllo on work surface. Spray pastry with butter-flavoured cooking spray. Cut into 4, 9 by 3 ½-inch strips. Place 1 tablespoon filling onto the lower corner of each strip. Fold phyllo over the filling, continuing to fold like a flag. Place triangles on parchment paper-lined baking sheet. Spray with cooking spray. Bake at 375°F for 10 to 12 minutes.

Note: These freeze really well. Simply put the pastries, on a cookie sheet, right into the freezer. Once they are frozen, put them in a heavy duty plastic storage bag and put them back in the freezer. When you want to cook them, preheat the oven and place the pastries on non-stick cookie sheets and increase baking time by 5 to 6 minutes.

Chive and Garlic Spread

2 cups grated Havarti cheese
1 (8 oz) (250 g) pkg cream cheese
2 tbsp whipping cream
1 small garlic clove, chopped

½ tsp dry mustard
¼ tsp pepper
3 tbsp chopped chives
4 tsp chopped parsley

In a food processor, purée together cheeses, cream, garlic, mustard and pepper until smooth. Stir in chives and parsley. Line a small, deep bowl with plastic wrap. Scrape mixture into bowl, pressing down firmly and smoothing top. Cover with plastic wrap and refrigerate until firm, about 2 hours. Unwrap and invert on serving plate, dusting with a few parsley leaves. Serve with assorted crackers.

Baba Ghannoush

When my daughter's family was in Edmonton, her best friend was middle eastern and she made this recipe for us one evening. It remains one of the best appetizers I've even eaten. Make sure you use good quality tahini – it keeps forever in the fridge but probably needs to be brought to room temperature before using.

1 large eggplant
2 to 3 cloves garlic, peeled
1 tsp salt
2 oz (4 tbsp) tahini (sesame butter)

2 tbsp yogurt or sour cream
Juice of 1 lemon
Olive oil and parsley for garnish

Roast halved or sliced eggplant on sprayed cookie sheet, at 425°F until tender. When cool enough to handle, remove peel and stem. Mash with fork or in food processor. Crush garlic with salt; add garlic, tahini and yogurt to mashed eggplant. Blend well and add lemon juice. Pour into serving dish and garnish with a drizzle of olive oil and parsley. Serve with baked pita chips.

Mexican Layer Dip

2 (14 oz) (396 ml) cans refried beans
Salsa
2 chopped avocados

8 oz (1 cup) sour cream
Chopped tomatoes
Grated cheddar cheese

Layer ingredients in order given. Garnish with sliced black olives. Serve with round taco chips to scoop.

Tiny Salmon Cake with Lemon Caper Mayonnaise

LEMON CAPER MAYONNAISE

½ cup mayonnaise
2 tbsp freshly squeezed lemon juice
1 tbsp drained capers
1 tbsp chopped fresh dill
Pinch cayenne pepper

Combine ingredients and refrigerate until ready to use.

SALMON CAKES

¼ cup finely chopped onion
¼ cup packed fresh parsley leaves
1 egg
2 tbsp grated lemon zest
1½ cup soft breadcrumbs
2 tbsp freshly squeezed lemon juice
2 tbsp butter, melted
1 tbsp Dijon mustard
½ tsp hot pepper sauce
1 lb (454 g) skinless salmon fillet, cooked, about 2 ½ cups
Salt
Pepper
1½ cup panko (fine, hard bread crumbs)
Vegetable oil

In a food processor, pulse onions and parsley until finely chopped. Add egg, fresh breadcrumbs, lemon zest, lemon juice, butter, mustard and hot pepper sauce. Pulse until well combined. Add salmon and pulse to combine. Transfer to bowl and season to taste. Cover and refrigerate overnight. Shape heaping teaspoonfuls of salmon mixture into small patties. Place panko in shallow dish (or on a sheet of waxed paper). Roll salmon patties to coat. In large skillet over medium heat, fry patties for about 2 minutes on each side until golden. Transfer to papertowel-lined plate to remove any excess oil. Place on a baking sheet in a low oven to keep warm until all are cooked. Serve with the lemon caper mayonnaise.

Asparagus Chicken Puffs

1 large chicken breast, cooked
2 tbsp mayonnaise
½ to 1 tsp curry powder
Salt
Pepper

1 (14 oz) (396 g) pkg puff pastry
½ lb (225 g) asparagus, steamed
1 egg, beaten
Sesame seeds, toasted

In a food processor, mix chicken, mayonnaise, curry, salt and pepper until smooth. Roll pastry into rectangle. Cut lengthwise into 3 even strips. Spread chicken mixture on one long side. Place asparagus lengthwise beside. Brush edges with egg. Roll pastry over to cover completely. Brush with egg. Cut into 1-inch pieces. Sprinkle with sesame seeds. Bake at 450°F for 10 minutes; lower heat to 350°F and bake for another 10 minutes until golden.

Sausage Balls

This recipe came off the box of biscuit mix. It's so simple but you have to knead it for 5 or more minutes to get everything mixed in. Once they are rolled into balls, you can put them on a cookie sheet and freeze them, which makes them individually frozen. When solidly frozen, remove to freezer bags and bake from frozen, adding about 7 to 10 minutes or until you see the cheese melting.

3 cups dry biscuit mix
1 lb (454 g) grated old cheddar

1 lb (454 g) ground sausage meat, hot Italian or whatever style you prefer

Combine all ingredients and knead until it comes together in a ball. Roll into 1-inch balls and bake at 400°F for 10 minutes or until golden brown.

Jalapeno Jelly

3 green peppers, seeded and chopped
2 (3½ oz) (100 ml) cans jalapeno peppers, with seeds
1½ cups vinegar
6 cups sugar
½ tsp cayenne (optional)
1 (6 oz) (180 ml) bottle pectin
4 to 6 drops green food coloring

Chop peppers and combine with vinegar in blender or food processor. Combine pepper mixture with sugar and cayenne. In a medium saucepan, bring to boil over medium heat. Add pectin according to package directions. Remove from heat. Skim off foam. Pour into hot sterilized jars and seal. Serve over a block of cream cheese with plenty of crackers.

Salmon Mousse

This also is a recipe from Rosemary – I can still taste how good it is.

2 (5 oz) (140 g) cans red salmon
1 tbsp unflavoured gelatin
¼ cup water
1 tbsp sugar
½ tsp chili sauce
¼ tbsp lemon juice

1 tbsp horseradish
1 tbsp mayonnaise
½ cup whipping cream
Salt
Pepper
Gherkins for garnish

Place salmon in a food processor and process. Sprinkle gelatin over cold water, heat in microwave on high to dissolve. In food processor, add sugar, chili sauce, lemon juice, horseradish, mayo and gelatin. Purée with whipped cream, beaten to soft peaks. Season with salt and pepper. Pour into oiled mold. Chill. Remove the mousse from the mold and slice several gherkins thinly over top to resemble scales. Serve with crudités or crackers.

Onion and Olive Crostini

2 onions, sliced
1 tbsp fresh thyme
2 cloves garlic, crushed
1 tbsp fresh oregano
3 tbsp olive oil
½ tsp balsamic vinegar

2 tbsp chopped black olives
Salt
Pepper
Anchovies and black olives
   for garnish

CROSTINI
12 thin slices baguette
Olive oil

Brush slices with olive oil. Bake 10 to 12 minutes, until golden.

Combine onions and garlic with oil, spices and olives in skillet. Cook over medium heat about 20 minutes, until soft. Stir in vinegar and season with salt and pepper. Spread onion mixture on baguette slices and decorate with anchovies and black olives.

John's Paté

1½ lb (680 g) chicken livers
1 cup onion, chopped

¾ lb (340 g) Oktoberfest sausage, skinned

Grind in food grinder or chop in food processor.

Transfer to large bowl and mix in the following
¾ cup chopped parsley
⅛ tsp thyme
2 tsp salt

½ cup butter, melted
¾ tsp pepper
2 eggs

CRUST
6 cups all purpose flour
2 tsp salt

1½ cups shortening
2 eggs

Work flour, shortening and salt together with fingers or food processor until it is the consistency of coarse crumbs. Make a well in the centre and add 2 eggs, one at a time, working the eggs into the pastry mixture. Gradually add 1½ cups of cold water. Add more or less cold water as necessary to make a smooth dough. Cover and let rest 1 hour. Roll out pastry dough and line a long loaf pan with it. Crimp edges; cut off excess. Egg-wash edges. Fill with chicken liver mixture. Add top crust, crimp edges and add two chimneys. Bake at 300°F for approximately 2 hours.

Jalapeno Pie

3 fresh green jalapeno peppers, slivered
6 eggs

1 lb (454 g) grated cheddar cheese
Dash of garlic powder and salt

Seed and sliver peppers. Spray a 9-inch baking pan with non-stick cooking spray and arrange slivered peppers on bottom of pan. Grate cheese over all. Beat eggs with dash of garlic powder and salt. Pour over slivered peppers and cheese. Bake at 350°F for about 30 minutes or until set. Cut into squares. Serve warm.

Cheddar Beer Spread

1 lb (454 g) grated cheddar cheese
½ tsp salt
2 cloves garlic
Pepper
1 tsp Tabasco
1 tsp paprika
1 tbsp Worcestershire sauce
1 tsp dry mustard
½ cup beer

Place all ingredients in food processor and process until coarsely blended. Refrigerate overnight. Serve with crackers.

Cream Cheese Oyster Spread

1 (85 g) can smoked oysters
1 (8 oz) (250 g) pkg cream cheese
1½ tbsp butter
1 tsp Worcestershire sauce
½ tsp garlic powder
½ tsp onion salt
Salt, to taste

Process above ingredients, except oysters, in food processor until well blended. Spread mixture out onto non-stick foil. Chop smoked oysters and lay on top of half the cheese mixture. Roll up so ends meet. Wrap tightly in foil and refrigerate at least 2 hours.

Artichoke Nibblers

14 oz (396 ml) artichoke hearts (cut in half if large)
½ cup mayonnaise
½ cup parmesan cheese

Place artichokes on a baking sheet lined with parchment paper. Place close enough together so they stand up. Place a teaspoon of mayonnaise on each, then sprinkle with parmesan. Broil about 2 minutes or until lightly browned.

Jelly Balls

1 lb (454 g) lean ground beef
1 egg, beaten
½ cup fine bread crumbs
2 tbsp parsley
½ cup chopped onion
1 tsp Worcestershire sauce
Salt
Pepper

SAUCE
12 oz (354 ml) chili sauce
10 oz (295 ml) grape jelly
1 tsp lemon juice
1 tbsp soy sauce

Bring sauce ingredients to a boil. Make up meatballs. Drop meatballs into sauce and simmer 30 minutes.

Samosas in Phyllo

1 cup cooked potato, peeled and diced
1 tsp oil
1 onion, chopped
2 tsp curry powder
2 tsp cumin
1 tsp turmeric
Dash salt
Pinch cayenne
½ lb (225 g) lean ground beef
½ cup frozen peas
1 tbsp lemon juice
9 sheets phyllo pastry
¼ cup melted butter (or use butter-flavoured cooking spray)

Cook onion in oil until softened. Stir in seasonings, cook 2 minutes more. Add beef, breaking up well. Mash potatoes coarsely, add to beef along with peas and lemon juice and enough broth to moisten. Cool. Lay 1 sheet phyllo on work surface. Brush with butter or spray with cooking spray. Cut into 3-inch strips. Spoon 1 tablespoon of filling along bottom. Fold up like a flag. Repeat. Bake for 20 minutes at 375°F. These freeze really well – place them on a cookie sheet in a single layer and put the cookie sheet in the freezer. When they are frozen, remove to a heavy-duty plastic bag and store in freezer. When you are ready to use them, place them on a cookie sheet and increase baking time by 5 minutes.

Grilled Scallops with Pancetta and Basil

This is a very elegant appetizer. It is easy to do and can be prepared ahead of time, except to put it on the skewers. They must be well soaked or they will burn.

1 bulb fennel
12 scallops
3 oz (85 g) pancetta
12 fresh basil leaves
¼ cup extra virgin olive oil
1 tsp chili flakes
1 tsp chopped garlic
6 bamboo skewers
Salt
Pepper

Soak skewers in hot water for 30 minutes. Cut fennel into 12 cubes. Cut pancetta into 12 cubes. Add chili flakes and garlic to olive oil. Place scallops, fennel and basil leaves on skewers. Brush with oil mixture and season with salt and pepper. Grill or broil for 2 minutes on high.

Salmon Terrine

- 1 lb (454 g) skinless Atlantic salmon
- ½ lb (225 g) smoked salmon, chopped
- 2 tbsp chopped fresh parsley
- 1 small red onion, finely chopped
- 2 tsp fresh dill and more for garnish
- ½ cup soft butter
- ¼ cup mayonnaise
- 2 tbsp grainy Dijon mustard
- 2 tbsp lemon juice
- Salt
- Pepper
- Crackers or bread

Roast salmon in 400°F oven for 10 minutes per inch of thickness. Cool and flake with a fork. In a large bowl, combine smoked salmon, parsley, onion and dill with fresh salmon. In a separate bowl, combine butter, mayonnaise, mustard, lemon juice, salt and pepper. Mix well. Line a 1-quart loaf pan with plastic wrap. Combine the two mixtures and turn into loaf pan. Gently press down with spatula to remove any air bubbles. Cover and refrigerate until firm. Remove from mold and serve with crackers or slices of whole grain baguette.

Mediterranean Layer Dip

- 8 oz (250 g) cream cheese, softened
- ½ cup mayonnaise
- 8 oz (227 ml) hummus
- 1 small tomato, seeded and finely chopped
- ½ cup finely chopped English cucumber
- ¼ cup feta with oregano

Mix mayonnaise with cream cheese. Spread onto serving platter. Top with remaining ingredients in order given. Serve with fresh vegetables and pita chips.

Olive and Cheddar Balls

½ cup butter
1 cup grated sharp cheddar cheese
1¼ cup flour
¼ tsp salt
¼ tsp paprika
Stuffed manzanilla olives

In a large bowl, cream together butter and cheese. Add flour and seasonings. Add enough water to make a smooth dough. Take a tablespoon or so of dough and form it into a saucer in the palm of your hand. Place olive in dough and wrap dough completely around the olive to seal it in. Place on greased or parchment paper-lined cookie sheet. Bake at 400°F for about 12 minutes or until golden. Serve warm.

Savoury Cheddar Cheesecake

8 oz (250 g) cream cheese, at room temperature
1 egg
½ cup shredded old cheddar
1 shallot, finely chopped
¼ tsp each cayenne pepper and smoked paprika
½ cup toasted pecans
½ cup peach chutney

Stir pecans with chutney. Remove half of the mixture and set aside. Beat cream cheese until softened. At low speed, beat in egg, scraping sides of bowl often. Beat in cheddar, shallot, cayenne and paprika. Stir half the chutney mixture into batter. Scrape mixture into parchment paper-lined 5-inch springform pan. Spread reserved chutney mixture over top. Centre pan on large sheet of heavy duty foil folded to come up sides of pan. Set springform pan into a larger pan. Into the larger pan, pour enough very hot water to come 1 inch up sides. Bake in a 300°F oven until the shine disappears and the edges are set, but the centre is still jiggling, about 1 ½ hours. Turn off oven. Run a knife around the edges of the pan. Let cool in oven for 1 hour. Remove springform pan from water. Transfer to rack and cool completely. Refrigerate until set and chilled, about 2 hours.

SOUPS, SALADS and SIDES

I love soups, could have them everyday for lunch. It is always nice to have salads with them, so I've included them in the same section. Most soups can be successfully frozen but don't freeze them with potatoes or pasta, they get soggy. If you are going to freeze the soup, add the cooked potato or pasta just before serving.

Oriental Slaw

SLAW

2 (170 g) pkgs ramen noodle mix, broken up (discard seasoning)	1 lb (454 g) package coleslaw mix OR 4 cups shredded cabbage
½ cup sunflower seeds or pumpkin seeds	2 tbsp diced green pepper
	2 tbsp diced green onion

DRESSING

½ cup sugar ⅓ cup cider vinegar
½ cup oil

Mix all ingredients and toss together. Let stand 15 minutes to soften noodles.

Cool Cucumber Gazpacho

⅓ cup chicken broth Pepper
3 cloves garlic, crushed 1 seedless green cucumber
¼ tsp cumin 2 chopped green onions
1 tbsp olive oil 2 tbsp chopped cilantro
1 tbsp lime juice 1 tbsp chopped mint
1 tsp sugar 1 cup no-fat yogurt
Salt

Combine broth, garlic and cumin. Simmer 3 minutes. Let cool. Whisk in olive oil, lime juice, sugar, salt and pepper. Chill. Chop or dice cucumber. Drain broth mixture, discarding solids. Add green onions, coriander and mint, toss to combine. Stir in yogurt, add salt and pepper to taste. Cover and chill. For smoother texture, purée.

Autumn Greens with Tamari Walnuts

This is a very elegant salad to serve and most of it can be done ahead. I do the walnuts early in the day, make the dressing and then assemble the salad at serving time.

TAMARI WALNUTS

1 tbsp tamari sauce	Pinch cayenne pepper
2 tsp molasses	1 cup walnuts
Pinch salt	

Preheat oven to 350°F. Stir together tamari, molasses, salt and cayenne pepper. Add nuts and toss to coat. Transfer to wire rack on foil-lined baking sheet and roast 10 minutes, until browned.

DRESSING

½ cup apple juice	¾ cup dried cherries
½ cup balsamic vinegar	1 tsp extra virgin olive oil

Bring apple juice and vinegar to a boil; pour over cherries and let stand for 30 minutes. Pour cherries into a strainer, reserving liquid. Set cherries aside. Reheat liquid to boiling, then reduce heat to simmer and cook for 15 minutes or until juice is reduced to about a quarter of its original volume. Mix liquid with extra virgin olive oil. Cool.

SALAD

9 oz (250 g) mixed field greens	1 cup crumbled Stilton cheese
1 small sliced onion	(or extra old cheddar)

To make the salad, mix field greens with tamari walnuts, onion, cheese and cherries. Whisk dressing and toss with salad.

Steak Soup

2 tbsp canola oil
2 tbsp butter
¼ cup chopped onion
2½ lb (1 kg) round steak, finely diced
3 tbsp flour
1 tbsp paprika
1 tsp salt
¼ tsp pepper
4 cups beef stock

2 cups water
1 large bay leaf
2 large stalks celery, including leaves, chopped
4 sprigs parsley
½ tsp marjoram
1½ cups cubed potato
1½ cups cubed carrots
¼ cup tomato paste

Heat butter and oil in a large skillet. Add onion and stir for about 5 minutes. Flour meat well and add to skillet, in batches, until browned. Add stock and water. Stir, scraping brown bits off the bottom of the pan. Add paprika, salt and pepper, then seasonings and vegetables. Turn heat to low and simmer 1 to 1½ hours or until vegetables and meat are tender. Stir in tomato paste, simmer another 15 minutes. Serve hot.

Squash and Apple Soup

1½ lb (566 g) butternut squash, peeled and cut into 1-inch cubes
1 tbsp olive oil
1½ tsp sugar

Toss squash cubes with olive oil and sugar. Place on parchment paper-lined baking sheet and bake at 400°F for 25 to 30 minutes. Set aside while you prepare the soup base.

SOUP BASE

2 tbsp olive oil
1 medium onion, chopped
1 clove garlic, minced
1 tbsp fresh thyme
1 medium onion, chopped
2 tart apples, peeled and cut into 1-inch pieces
1 qt (1 L) chicken broth
½ cup roasted pumpkin seeds, optional
Fresh ground black pepper
1 to 2 cups water
2 tbsp brown sugar

Brown onion and garlic in olive oil. Cook until tender. Add remaining ingredients, except pumpkin seeds and bring to simmer. Add squash and cook until apples are tender, about 15 minutes. Purée with immersion blender. Add enough water to thin to desired consistency. Add brown sugar and stir. Garnish with toasted pumpkin seeds.

One of the things I've always been surprised at is the scope of viewers to our show. It seems every time we go to Costco in Moncton, we run into fans. It's to the point that when we go, my daughter always says, "I wonder how many Kitchen stalkers will be here today." One day, at the checkout, a delightful couple addressed me and asked if I really was Joan McElman. I assured them I was. The fellow said they were fans who lived in Sackville, NB and that they were professors at Mount Allison University. He asked if we knew of his son: Ian Hanomansingh of CBC Television. Talk about a compliment.

Potato Soup

3 or 4 large baking potatoes, peeled and diced
Enough water to cover potatoes
1 large onion, diced
2 stalks celery, diced

1 carrot, peeled and diced
2 cups chicken broth
1 cup milk
2 tbsp flour
Old cheddar cheese, shredded

In a large saucepan, bring water and vegetables to a boil. Decrease heat and simmer until vegetables are tender. Add chicken broth. Purée with immersion blender. Mix milk with flour. Add to broth and stir until slightly thickened. Serve with a garnish of old cheddar cheese.

One thing to remember when puréeing soup is if you're not using an immersion blender, let it cool for at least 20 minutes before puréeing in a standard blender. Otherwise, the heat will blow the lid off.

Roasted Garlic, Turnip and Sweet Potato Soup

1 large sweet potato, peeled and diced
1 large turnip, peeled and diced
3 tbsp olive oil
8 cloves whole garlic, peeled
2 sliced shallots or
  ¼ cup diced onion

2 tsp fresh thyme (½ tsp dried)
4 cups chicken broth
½ cup white wine
1 tbsp balsamic vinegar
Low-fat Greek yogurt for garnish

Heat oven to 400°F. In a large bowl, toss sweet potato and turnip with 2 tbsp oil. Place vegetables on parchment paper-lined baking sheets and roast 15 minutes. In same bowl, toss garlic and shallots with remaining 1 tbsp oil. Add to pan and stir everything to turn. Roast 20 minutes longer. In large saucepan, bring broth and wine to simmer, add roasted vegetables and cook 10 minutes. Purée using immersion blender. Add vinegar, salt and pepper to taste. Garnish with a dollop of Greek yogurt.

Curried Apple Soup

My husband brought this recipe home from a dinner he attended in Jacksonville, Fla. He was so impressed and I've been using it for years. Another one that can be made well ahead and just reheated at the last minute.

3 tbsp butter
1 large onion, diced
4 stalks celery, chopped
4 large apples, peeled, cored and cut in quarters
Juice of 1 lemon
2 cups chicken broth
1 cup beef broth
2 cups water
2 tsp curry powder
1 cup cream (may use heavy cream or coffee cream)

In a large saucepan, sauté onion and celery in butter over medium heat for about 10 minutes, until onion is soft. Add apples. Simmer for about 15 minutes or until apples are soft. Add curry powder, both broths, lemon juice and water. Purée with immersion blender; strain out any solids. Add cream just before serving.

This can be made ahead and frozen, or chilled and reheated before serving. When reheating, bring to a simmer, add cream and serve. May also be served cold.

Country Ham Chowder

2 medium potatoes, diced
3 tbsp butter
¾ cup finely chopped onion
¼ cup chopped carrots
½ cup chopped celery
3 tbsp flour
2½ to 3 cups milk
Dash salt and pepper
2 tbsp Dijon mustard
1 cup finely chopped ham
1 cup grated cheddar

Simmer potatoes in ¾ cup water until almost tender, about 10 minutes. Melt butter in large saucepan, add onion, carrot and celery and sauté until soft. Stir in flour and cook 2 minutes, stirring well. Add milk, potatoes and water; then add salt, pepper and mustard. Bring to simmer, add ham and cheese, stir until cheese melts.

Iowa Corn Chowder

This recipe was from an Iowa State Senator's wife, who gave us a guided tour of the White House in Washington, DC. It was served in the Senate Dining Room, the most exclusive dining room in Washington.

¼ lb (113 g) bacon
1 cup water
1 large onion, chopped
2 (15 oz) (445 ml) cans corn
1 cup celery, diced
2 cups milk
4 cups potatoes, peeled and diced
1 (14 oz) (414 ml) can evaporated milk
Salt
Pepper
Cayenne pepper (optional)

In a large saucepan, brown the bacon. Remove bacon from pan. Pour off all but 2 tablespoons of bacon fat. Sauté onion and celery in bacon fat for 5 minutes. Add potatoes and water, cook over medium heat, about 10 minutes or until potatoes are done. Stir in corn. Add milk and evaporated milk to chowder. Season with salt and pepper. Add cayenne pepper if you like.

My Mother's Ukrainian Borscht

Most borscht recipes are meatless but mom used to use this as a replacement for the dinner meal. You can omit the steak if you desire.

1½ lb (600 g) round steak, diced small
1 tbsp oil
1 cup water
4 cups shredded cabbage
2 cups shredded beets (I use canned beets and shred them)
2 medium tomatoes, peeled, seeded and chopped
1 cup diced carrots
½ cup chopped onion
1 tbsp sugar
1½ tsp cider vinegar
1 qt (1 L) beef broth
½ cups cubed peeled potato
2 tbsp tomato paste
1 tbsp each chopped parsley and dill
½ tsp salt and dash pepper
½ cup sour cream, for garnish

In a four-quart saucepan, heat oil. Add meat and brown, in batches, if necessary, until all are browned. Carefully add water, scraping up browned bits from bottom of the pan. Add vegetables, sugar, beef stock and vinegar. Bring to a boil. Reduce heat and simmer for about 1 hour. Stir in remaining ingredients, except for sour cream and cook until potatoes are tender. Ladle into bowls and garnish with sour cream and fresh dill.

When we were first doing the cooking show in Aylesford, we had a pretty small space. The first studio was set up with a brick façade behind the work area. One day we were making borscht. I put it in the blender, then turned my back to the machine to talk to the camera. The counter the blender was on was uneven, I assume, because the blender bounced right off the counter and hit the wall, splattering red goop all over the wall, the floor and me. Some clean-up that day! Good thing I always carried an extra top — never knew when I'd need it.

Spicy Black Bean Soup

1 large red onion, diced
1 medium red pepper, diced
1 jalapeno pepper, seeded and diced
2 tbsp olive oil
3 cloves garlic, minced
3 (15 oz) (445 ml) cans black beans, drained and rinsed
4 cups chicken or vegetable broth
1 (14 oz) (398 ml) can diced tomatoes
2 cans chopped green chilies
⅓ cup sherry or additional stock
2 tbsp minced fresh cilantro
½ cup sour cream
¼ cup grated old cheddar

In a large saucepan, sauté onions and peppers in oil until tender. Add garlic and cook 1 minute more. Stir in beans, broth, tomatoes and green chilies. Bring to a boil. Reduce heat and simmer, uncovered, for 25 minutes. Add sherry and cilantro. Cook 5 minutes longer. Remove from heat and let cool slightly. Place half the soup in a blender and purée. Return to the pan and heat thoroughly. Top each serving with 2 teaspoons of sour cream and 1 teaspoon of cheese.

Acorn Squash and Pear Soup

2 medium acorn squash, peeled and cut into 1-inch cubes
4 medium, firm pears, peeled and coarsely chopped
2 stalks celery, thinly sliced
1 onion, finely chopped
2 tbsp butter, melted
1 tsp dried thyme
1 tsp salt
½ tsp dried sage
½ tsp pepper
4 cups chicken broth

In a large bowl, combine first 5 ingredients and toss to coat. Transfer to shallow roasting pan (or parchment paper-lined cookie sheet). Roast at 375°F for 1 to 1¼ hours or until squash is tender, stirring occasionally. Cool slightly. In a food processor, process squash mixture with broth until mixture is smooth. Transfer to a large pot and heat thoroughly.

French Onion Soup

10 medium yellow onions, halved, peeled and sliced
2 tbsp olive oil
2 tbsp sugar
1 tsp dried thyme
Coarse salt and pepper
2 qt (2 L) beef broth
¾ cup red wine
French bread
Grated Swiss cheese

Preheat oven to 450°F. In a large roasting pan, combine onions, oil, sugar, thyme, 2 teaspoons of salt and a dash of pepper. Cover tightly with lid and cook until steamed about 30 minutes. Uncover and cook, stirring every 10 minutes until onions are golden brown (30 to 60 minutes). Transfer mixture to a large pot, add broth and 6 cups of water. Bring to a boil, then reduce heat and simmer. Cook until liquid has darkened, about 20 minutes. Meanwhile, deglaze roasting pan with wine, scraping up all browned bits from pan. Simmer 2 to 3 minutes. Pour into broth mixture. Season with salt and pepper. To serve, first divide soup evenly between bowls. Toast slices of French bread until just golden. Top bread with grated Swiss cheese and broil until cheese melts. Top bowls of soup with bread slices.

This recipe makes a huge amount. You can either freeze it in containers for future use, or cut the recipe in half.

Creamy Leek Soup with Brie

2½ cups chopped leeks, white part only
2 tbsp butter
2½ cups chicken stock
2 cups light cream
¼ cup flour
Salt
Pepper
8 oz (227 g) Brie
2 tbsp chopped fresh chives

Clean leeks by cutting the stalk in half and spreading the layers in water to wash out any remaining sand. Cut off white parts and slice. Sauté in butter until tender. Add broth, bring to a boil and cover. Reduce heat and simmer for 20 minutes. Strain, reserving broth in the pan. Place leeks in a blender with ½ the chicken stock and process until smooth. Return to pan and stir in 1 ½ cups of cream. Combine flour, salt, pepper and remaining cream until smooth. Stir into soup. Cook 1 to 2 minutes. Reduce heat to low. Cut brie into small pieces and add to soup gradually until cheese is melted. Garnish with chives.

Watermelon Salsa

This is a great recipe to serve with fish or chicken. It perks up the colour and gives a great piquant touch to it.

4 cups chopped seedless watermelon
2 tbsp fresh lime juice
1 tbsp chopped cilantro
1 tbsp finely chopped red onion
2 tsp jalapeno, seeded and finely chopped
Salt

Combine all ingredients in a large bowl. Refrigerate one hour before serving.

Watermelon Gazpacho

A delightful recipe in the summer, so nice and colourful and so cool. Great way to use up the watermelon.

GAZPACHO

8 cups chopped seedless watermelon
1 tbsp sherry vinegar
2 tbsp lime juice
1 tbsp olive oil
1 tsp Sriracha sauce
Salt
1 cup diced cucumber
1 cup diced red onion
1 cup diced yellow pepper

YOGURT GARNISH

⅓ cup plain yogurt
1 tbsp lime juice
¼ tsp grated lime zest
2 tbsp chopped fresh mint

Purée six cups of watermelon in a food processor or a blender. Dice remaining watermelon into ¼-inch pieces. Stir in sherry vinegar, lime juice, olive oil and Sriracha sauce. Season with salt to taste. Pour mixture into a large bowl; add cucumber, onion and pepper. Cover and chill well. Serve in chilled bowls and top with yogurt garnish.

Gazpacho

4 or 5 ripe tomatoes, peeled, or 1 (28 oz) (796 ml) can diced tomatoes
½ onion, chopped
½ green pepper, chopped
½ English cucumber, chopped
2 cups vegetable juice
Salt and pepper, if needed
Dash Worcestershire sauce

In a blender, add all ingredients and blend until you have the consistency you like – if you like it chunkier, just barely blend. Chill. Serve with a few small pieces of cucumber and croutons for garnish.

Roasted Cauliflower Soup with Cheddar Crostini

1 head cauliflower, cut into 2-inch pieces
1 tbsp vegetable oil
2 tbsp butter
2 leeks, white and light green parts only, halved and sliced
2 cloves garlic, minced
2 qt (2 L) chicken broth
1½ cups water
Pepper and salt
1½ cups grated old cheddar cheese
1 tbsp Dijon mustard

Place cauliflower on parchment paper-lined baking sheet. Drizzle with oil. Roast in a 425°F oven, turning occasionally, until very deep golden brown on all sides (about 45 minutes). Meanwhile, melt butter in skillet. Cook leeks and garlic in melted butter, stirring until leeks have softened, about 6 minutes. In a blender, purée (in batches if necessary) until smooth the cauliflower, leek mixture and broth. Transfer to a large pot, stir in water, salt and pepper. Bring to a boil, reduce heat and stir in cheese and mustard. Simmer until cheese has melted.

CHEDDAR CROSTINI

¾ cup grated extra-old cheddar
2 tsp chopped fresh parsley
4 tsp Dijon mustard
16 ½-inch thick slices of baguette

Mix cheese with parsley, spread mustard over baguette slices and top with cheese mixture. Bake on parchment paper-lined baking sheet until cheese is melted and bread is golden. Let stand 2 minutes. Serve with soup.

Pumpkin Bisque with Smoked Gouda

4 strips bacon, chopped
1 medium onion, chopped
3 cloves garlic, minced
6 cups chicken broth
1 (28 oz) (796 ml) can solid pack pumpkin
¼ tsp salt
¼ tsp nutmeg
¼ tsp pepper
1 cup cream
1 cup shredded smoked gouda
2 tbsp chopped fresh parsley
Additional shredded smoked gouda for garnish

Cook the bacon until crisp. Remove to paper towel. Reserve 1 tablespoon of bacon drippings. Sauté onion in bacon drippings for 1 minute; add garlic and cook 1 minute longer. Stir in broth, pumpkin, salt, nutmeg and pepper. Bring to a boil, reduce heat and simmer for 10 minutes, uncovered. Let cool for 10 minutes or so. In a blender or a food processor, process soup in batches until smooth. Return to pot; stir in cream. Heat thoroughly but do not boil. Add cheese and stir until melted. Sprinkle each serving with parsley, bacon and additional shredded cheese.

Salad à la Carolyn

1 tsp salt
½ tsp dry mustard
3 tbsp vinegar
1 tbsp honey

3 tbsp toasted sesame seeds
Greens as desired, e.g. spinach, romaine lettuce, butter lettuce

Mix together salt, mustard, vinegar and honey. Brown 3 tablespoons sesame seeds in a dry pan (or in 300°F oven for 5 to 10 minutes). Mix together lettuce, spinach and romaine. Toss with dressing and sprinkle with toasted sesame seeds.

Watermelon, Feta and Black Olive Salad

1 small red onion
Bunch of fresh mint, chopped
2 to 4 limes, juiced (½ cup)
3 to 4 tbsp olive oil

3 lb (1.5 kg) watermelon, peeled and diced
3½ oz (100 g) pitted black olives
8 oz (250 g) feta cheese
Black pepper

Peel and halve onion. Cut into fine slices. Steep onion in lime juice. Peel watermelon and dice, or cut into triangular, bite-sized pieces. Cut feta into similar pieces. Place in glass bowl. Tear leaves off parsley as well as mint. Add onions, olives and oil; toss gently to coat. Add a good grind of fresh black pepper.

Corn and Black Bean Salsa

½ cup medium salsa
½ cup green pepper, chopped
1 (14 oz) (414 ml) can corn, drained
1 to 2 tsp chili powder

1 (14 oz) (414 ml) can black beans, drained and rinsed
Finely chopped cilantro

Combine all ingredients. Add enough chili powder to flavour. Add Tabasco sauce if you want more heat.

Curried Shrimp and Grape Salad

2 cups cooked shrimp
4 cups green grapes, halved
2 cups unsalted cashews

½ cup chopped celery
½ cup minced green onions

DRESSING

1 cup mayonnaise
¼ tsp ginger
1 cup sour cream

2 tbsp lemon juice
1 tbsp curry powder
Salt and pepper

Make sure shrimp is cool and dry. Toss ingredients with everything but cashews. Toss with dressing and top with cashews just before serving.

This is a great salad for lunch, but for a little more interest, stuff halved pita pockets with the mixture.

Tabbouleh

This recipe is an original one from my daughter, who got it from her best friend, who is from Lebanon. Tabbouleh is a staple of the Lebanese diet.

1 cup bulgur
1 cup water
1 bunch green onions, finely chopped
1½ cups finely chopped parsley
½ cup olive oil
1 tsp salt

½ cup lemon juice
½ tsp pepper
2 or 3 tomatoes, seeded and chopped
½ cup chopped mint
½ cup cucumber, diced

Soak bulgur in water for 30 minutes. Drain through a strainer. Press with paper towels to soak up any residual liquid. In a large bowl, combine bulgur with green onions, parsley, oil, salt, lemon juice, mint and pepper. Add tomatoes and cucumber just before serving.

Oriental Romaine Salad

I make up the whole recipe of the noodle mixture and the whole dressing recipe. Then for the two of us, I tear the amount of lettuce we need, then top with ¼ of the noodles and dressing.

½ cup slivered almonds
½ cup sunflower seeds
1 pkg (85 g) Oriental ramen noodles and half the seasonings
¼ cup melted butter

Brown together, set on paper towels to drain and let cool:

DRESSING
1 cup oil
¼ cup sugar
¼ cup vinegar
2 tbsp soy sauce

Shake together in dressing bottle. Best if it stands for 30 minutes before using.

Tear two heads romaine lettuce into bite-size pieces. Make sure it is clean. Toss with noodle mixture and dressing.

Broccoli and Mandarin Salad

DRESSING

2 eggs
¼ cup white sugar
¼ cup white vinegar
1 tsp cornstarch
1 tsp dry mustard
¼ cup water or juice from oranges
½ cup mayonnaise

Combine above ingredients, except mayonnaise, in a microwave-safe bowl and cook in the microwave for 2 minutes on high. Whisk until smooth. Cook 2 to 3 minutes more, whisking every minute until thickened. Cool. Whisk in mayonnaise.

SALAD

4 cups fresh broccoli florets
½ cup slivered almonds, toasted
½ cup raisins
1 can (284 ml) mandarin oranges, drained
8 slices bacon, cooked crisp and crumbled
½ red onion, sliced
2 cups sliced fresh mushrooms

Toss salad ingredients with dressing at serving time. Makes enough for 2 salads or will feed eight people easily.

Broccoli and Rice Casserole

½ cup butter
1 small onion, chopped
2 (10 oz) packages frozen chopped broccoli, thawed and squeezed dry

1 (10 oz) (284 ml) can cream of mushroom soup
¾ cup milk
¾ lb (340 g) process cheese, cubed
2 cups cooked rice

Melt butter, sauté onions. Add the broccoli and cook about 10 minutes. Add the soup, milk and cheese to broccoli mixture and cook 10 minutes, until the cheese is melted. Add the rice. Place in a buttered casserole dish and bake at 325°F for about 30 minutes.

I always like to have fresh vegetables and herbs. To keep celery fresh, wrap it tightly in heavy-duty foil as soon as you get it home from the market. It will keep in the fridge for three weeks. Each time you unwrap it, make sure to rewrap it tightly. If the foil breaks, put fresh on. To keep parsley and basil fresh, immerse the stem end in a measuring cup. Fill the cup half full with water and slide a sandwich bag over the top. Place it in the fridge and change the water every second day. It will keep fresh for at least a week.

Layered Lettuce Salad

1 head iceberg lettuce, shredded
1 cup celery, diced
1 to 2 chopped green onions
1 (10 oz) (300 ml) can water chestnuts, drained and sliced

2 cups frozen green peas, thawed but not cooked
2 cups mayonnaise
2 tbsp sugar
½ lb (225 g) mozzarella cheese, shredded

Layer ingredients in order given in a 9 by 13 inch glass casserole. Frost with mayonnaise. Sprinkle the sugar over. Cover with shredded mozzarella cheese. Refrigerate several hours or overnight.

Pear and Stilton Salad

DRESSING

¼ cup lemon juice
1 tbsp honey

¼ cup vegetable oil
2 tsp Dijon mustard

Whisk together and set aside.

SALAD

Butter lettuce
4 oz (100 g) Stilton cheese, crumbled

2 ripe pears, cored and sliced
¼ cup toasted pine nuts

Arrange lettuce on serving plates. Arrange pears over top. Sprinkle with cheese and pine nuts. Drizzle dressing over.

Cucumber Ring Supreme

1 tbsp sugar
1½ tsp unflavoured gelatin
½ tsp salt

2 tbsp lemon juice
¾ cup water
½ cup cucumber, thinly sliced

Dissolve sugar, gelatin and salt in ¼ cup water. Heat 30 seconds in microwave to dissolve. Add lemon juice. Pour into mold sprayed with cooking spray. Chill until partially set. Arrange cucumber slices on top of gelatin, overlapping slightly, pressing down into the gelatin mixture. Chill until set.

SECOND RING

2 tbsp sugar
1 envelope unflavoured gelatin
¾ tsp salt
2 tbsp lemon juice
1 (8 oz) (250 g) pkg cream cheese

2 English cucumbers, peeled and shredded
1 cup mayonnaise
¼ cup chopped parsley
3 tbsp finely chopped onion

Mix sugar, salt, gelatin and ¾ cup water. Heat in microwave until dissolved, stir in lemon juice. Gradually beat hot gelatin mixture into softened cream cheese until smooth. Measure out 2 cups of cucumbers. Press cucumbers into sieve and squeeze out as much moisture as possible. Add to cheese mixture. Fold in mayonnaise, parsley and onion. Pour into mold. Chill well. Unmold onto a bed of lettuce.

About a year after we were married, we were posted to CFB Namao (Edmonton). We moved into an as yet unfinished apartment building right across the hall from friends who were posted to the base at the same time. We had a two-week-old baby daughter in tow. As the spring turned into summer, several Edmonton Eskimo football players, some with families, moved into the building. One couple had a young son who frequently ran away from home. I used to leave my door ajar in case my neighbour came over while I was feeding the baby. Young Billy Joe used to pop in to see the baby. After about the third time, his mother didn't bother looking for him anymore — she'd just arrive at my door and ask, "Is he here?" Once the football games started, there were tailgate parties in the parking lot — lots of Texas BBQ, etc. Billy Joe's dad was a 6'6" tackle and weighed about 240 pounds. He would pick my daughter up and hold her in his big palm, her back resting on the heel of his hand and her bottom on his fingers. He loved to dance around the parking lot with this tiny girl.

Crunchy Pea Salad

2 cups frozen peas, thawed, not cooked
6 slices bacon, cooked and crumbled
½ cup chopped celery
½ cup chopped green onions
1 cup salted cashews, chopped

Mix peas, celery and green onions together.

DRESSING
½ cup sour cream
2 tbsp mayonnaise
½ tsp salt
Freshly ground black pepper.

Combine dressing ingredients and toss dressing with pea mixture. Top with bacon and cashews.

Sweet Potato Casserole

3 cups cooked, mashed sweet potatoes
1 cup brown sugar
1 tsp vanilla
⅓ cup butter, melted
2 eggs

Mix all ingredients together and put into a greased 9-inch pan.

TOPPING

1 cup brown sugar
⅓ cup flour
1 cup chopped pecans
½ cup butter

Mix topping ingredients together until crumbly. Sprinkle on top of potato mixture. Bake at 325°F for about 35 minutes or until hot all the way through. This can be assembled and frozen, but thaw before baking.

Twice Baked Potatoes

6 medium baking potatoes
1 tsp salt
½ tsp pepper
¼ cup butter
¼ cup milk
2 tbsp minced green onions or chives
4 oz (100 g) shredded cheddar cheese

Bake potatoes until done. Cut in half lengthwise. Scoop out inside, leaving ¼-inch shell for support. In a large bowl, mash pulp; add salt, pepper, butter, milk, onion and cheese. Reserve a bit of cheese for topping. Stir potato mixture together and spoon into potato shells. Place upright in a baking pan and sprinkle with reserved cheese. Bake at 350°F uncovered for 20 to 25 minutes.

Brazilian Cheese Rolls

This is a great gluten free recipe. They taste like cheesy popovers and are delicious both warm and cooled.

1 large egg, at room temperature
⅓ cup light olive oil or canola oil
⅔ cup whole milk
1½ cups tapioca flour
½ cup crumbled Mexican farmer's cheese (or old white cheddar)
1 tsp salt

Preheat oven to 400°F. Spray a 24 mini-muffin tin with cooking spray. Place all ingredients in a blender or a food processor, or use a handheld immersion blender. Pulse until smooth, scraping down sides of container to make certain everything is mixed. Pour into prepared muffin tins until almost level with top of each tin. Carefully place on the middle rack of the oven and bake 10 to 14 minutes or until puffy and golden brown. Remove from oven; let cool on wire rack 5 minutes, then turn muffin tin on its side and gently pull out rolls.

Sweet and Sour Green Beans

4 slices bacon
1 large onion, chopped
Salt
Pepper
1 lb (454 g) green beans, trimmed
¼ cup cider vinegar
2 tbsp sugar

In a skillet, cook bacon until browned. Transfer to paper towel-lined plate. Reserve pan drippings. Add onion to skillet. Season with salt and pepper. Cook, stirring until onion starts to brown, about 3 to 5 minutes. Add green beans with ¼ cup of water. Cook, stirring occasionally, until beans are tender, about 10 minutes. Crumble bacon into skillet. Add vinegar and bacon. Cook until syrupy sauce forms, about 2 minutes. Toss to coat.

Turnip and Squash Swirl

2 cups butternut or Hubbard squash
2 lb (1 kg) turnip
1½ cups water, divided
½ cup whipping cream
½ tsp salt, divided
2 tbsp butter
2 tbsp rum (optional)
½ cup chopped parsley

Peel, seed and cube squash, or poke holes in skin with skewer and microwave 4 to 5 minutes, then cool until you can handle it. Peel and cube turnip. Place each vegetable in a separate pan, with ¾ cup water each and cook about 20 minutes until tender when pierced with a knife. Drain vegetables, but keep separate. Purée turnip in a food processor. Add whipping cream and ¼ teaspoon of salt. Set aside. Purée squash in bowl and add butter, rum (if using) and ¼ teaspoon of salt. In a buttered baking dish, spoon in dollops of each mixture and then lightly swirl with tip of knife. Bake at 350°F for about 20 minutes. Sprinkle with parsley.

Gourmet Cranberry Sauce

12 oz (375 g) fresh cranberries
1 cup white sugar
1 whole orange, peeled and cut in chunks
2 tbsp Grand Marnier or any orange liqueur

In a blender or a food processor, process cranberries, sugar and orange until coarsely chopped. Add liqueur and chill until needed.

So much better than canned cranberry sauce and takes no time at all. Keeps for several weeks in the freezer. My guests have been known to serve it with ice cream for dessert.

Hot Curried Fruit

1 cup brown sugar
Salt
1 tbsp curry powder
½ cup butter

3 (14 oz) (398 ml) cans fruit of your choice (pears, peaches, apricots, mandarin oranges)

In a small saucepan, combine the first four ingredients. Bring to a boil. Pour over drained fruit and put into casserole. Bake at 350°F for 20 minutes. Serve in bowls, adding a few maraschino cherries for garnish. Delicious on its own, or poured over french vanilla ice cream as a sauce. This is a great side dish to serve with ham or chicken. For a smaller group, i.e. two people – use 1 (14 ounce) can fruit cocktail and cut down on the remaining ingredients.

Potatoes Romanoff

8 large potatoes, cooked and mashed
1½ cups shredded cheddar cheese, divided
20 oz (560 g) sour cream
1 bunch green onions, chopped
1½ tsp salt
Paprika

Mash potatoes; add remaining ingredients except for ½ cup cheese and paprika. Cool and freeze, if desired. When ready to use, thaw in microwave and cook on stovetop 8 to 10 minutes, stirring several times, or bake in the oven at 400°F for 30 minutes. Top with cheese and continue cooking until cheese melts. Garnish with a dusting of paprika. This recipe has been a favorite for years. It makes enough for 8 to 10 people, but reheats quite well.

Buffet Potato Casserole

5 lb (2.25 kg) potatoes
8 oz (225 g) cream cheese, softened
1 cup sour cream
2 tsp onion salt
Pepper
2 tbsp melted butter

Cook and mash potatoes. Add other ingredients and beat until smooth. Place in buttered casserole and dot with butter. Bake at 350°F for 30 minutes. This recipe can be made early and reheated in time for dinner, or can be frozen. Simply thaw overnight in fridge and then bake as above, adding 10 minutes to baking time.

ENTREES

When we were newlyweds, everyone in our neighbourhood was in the same financial straights, so potluck was the only way we could entertain. A lot of these recipes are easily made ahead or ready to be reheated. However, as we got older and less stressed financially, we have always had dinners at our house. I love to entertain and you will always get good results with these recipes.

Chicken Breasts Stuffed with Asparagus

4 boneless skinless chicken breasts, pounded ½ inch thick
12 asparagus spears, lightly steamed
¼ cup butter, melted
2 tbsp Dijon mustard
2 cloves garlic, mashed
¼ cup white wine
1½ cups fine bread crumbs or panko
½ cup flour

Combine butter, mustard, garlic and wine. Place 3 pieces of asparagus on each chicken piece. Roll up and secure with toothpick. Dip into flour, then wine mixture, then breadcrumbs. Drizzle with melted butter. Bake 30 minutes at 350°F. Garnish with parsley.

For a simpler dinner, omit the asparagus and the wine and substitute water. Bake breaded, seasoned chicken breasts on a greased baking sheet at 400°F for about 15 minutes.

Chicken Bake

8 boneless skinless chicken breasts
8 slices bacon
4 oz (114 g) smoked meat
1 (10 oz) (284 ml) can cream of mushroom soup
1 cup sour cream

Wrap each chicken breast with bacon. Line a casserole dish with smoked meat. Lay chicken over. Mix mushroom soup and sour cream. Pour over the meat. Bake at 250°F for 4 to 5 hours. Also great in a slow cooker: cook about six hours on low or 2½ hours on high.

You can use smoked meat, pastrami or even black forest ham. One of few recipes that doesn't separate with long-time cooking.

Sweet and Spicy Cashew Chicken

SAUCE

½ cup ketchup
2 tbsp soy sauce
2 tbsp Worchestershire sauce
3 tbsp brown sugar
½ tsp sesame oil
½ cup chicken broth

Combine sauce ingredients and set aside.

2 tbsp cornstarch
dash salt
½ tsp sugar

Mix together in a zipper freezer bag.

1 ½ lb chicken breast, cut into 2-inch squares

Toss into bag and mix gently to coat each piece.

¼ cup vegetable oil
3 tbsp minced fresh ginger
1 tbsp minced garlic
1 small onion, chopped
2 red or orange peppers, diced
2 carrots, sliced on the diagonal
2 cups snow peas, remove strings and tips
1 ½ cup salted cashews
Toasted sesame seeds for garnish

Heat oil until ripples form. Add coated chicken, ginger and garlic. Stir fry until chicken is opaque (only about 1 minute). Add peppers and carrots and stir fry for 2 to 3 minutes until just barely tender. Add snow peas and reserved sauce, cook until thickened. Place on serving platter. Add cashews and sprinkle with sesame seeds.

My Favourite Chicken Casserole

2 cups cooked chicken, diced
1 cup celery, chopped
1 cup slivered almonds, toasted
2 cups cooked rice
1 cup mayonnaise
2 tbsp chopped onion
2 tbsp lemon juice

1 (10 oz) (284 ml) can cream of chicken soup
1 (10 oz) (284 ml) can cream of mushroom soup
1 chicken bouillon cube, dissolved in ½ cup water
Potato chips, crushed

Mix all ingredients together in an oven-proof casserole and top with crushed potato chips. Bake at 400°F for 30 to 40 minutes.

Mexican Turkey Casserole

1½ cups chopped turkey or chicken
4 oz (120 ml) can chopped green chilies
1½ cups chicken gravy (canned or leftover)

2 green onions, diced
8 oz (236 ml) sour cream
2 tbsp chopped black olives (optional)

In large mixing bowl, combine above ingredients.

1½ cup coarsely crushed corn chips

1½ cup grated old cheddar cheese

Have in reserve:

1 tomato, chopped
Shredded lettuce

Salsa

Grease sides of 1½ quart casserole. Sprinkle ⅓ of the corn chips over. Pour half the turkey mixture over, then top with half the cheese. Repeat layers, ending with the corn chips. Bake at 375°F for about 35 minutes or until heated through. Garnish with tomatoes, lettuce and salsa.

Spicy Sticky Chicken Wings

3 lb (1.5 kg) chicken wings, cut in two, discarding wingtips
⅓ cup each hoisin sauce, soy sauce and honey
2 tsp each minced garlic, grated ginger and hot pepper sauce

Arrange wings on a baking sheet lined with non-stick foil. Cook at 425°F for about 20 minutes, turning once. Meanwhile, combine other ingredients, bring to a boil and simmer 5 minutes. When wings are cooked, drain off any accumulated fat and pour the sauce ingredients over, turning wings to make sure each surface is coated. Reduce heat to 375°F and cook 20 minutes more, turning several times, until wings are sticky and shiny.

I guarantee you won't be able to keep up with the demand for these. They are addictive. They are equally good at room temperature but best served hot.

Turkey Paprika

1 medium onion, sliced
2 tbsp butter
2 tbsp flour
2 tsp paprika
1 cup chicken broth
2 slightly beaten egg yolks
1 cup sour cream
4 oz (113 g) sliced mushrooms, sautéed until liquid evaporates
2 cups diced turkey or chicken

In a large saucepan or deep skillet, cook onion and mushrooms in butter until tender. Set mushrooms aside. Blend in flour, paprika and ½ teaspoon of salt. Add broth and cook until mixture thickens. Cook 1 minute more. In a small bowl, stir a small amount of the liquid into egg yolks. Return egg mixture to hot skillet. Cook over low heat 1 minute more. Stir in sour cream until well blended. Add turkey and mushrooms. Heat but do not boil. Serve over hot cooked noodles.

Coq au Vin

3 tbsp each butter and vegetable oil
3½ lb (1.6 kg) cut up chicken (or use legs and thighs)
Seasoned flour
1 cup coarsely chopped onion
8 oz (226 g) fresh mushroom, left whole if small, cut in half if large
2 cloves garlic, crushed
¼ tsp thyme
2 sprigs parsley
1 bay leaf
Salt
Pepper
¼ cup brandy
1 cup red wine

Dredge chicken pieces in seasoned flour. In pan, melt butter and oil together. Add chicken and brown well on all sides. Pour chicken and juices into ovenproof casserole. Add onions, mushrooms and garlic to pan. Cook until mushrooms release their liquid. Add to casserole along with spices, salt and pepper. Warm brandy until it will light with a match. Pour hot brandy over chicken. Light with match. When flame burns down, add wine. Cover and bake in 350°F oven until chicken is tender, about 1 hour.

This recipe reheats very well and sometimes I make it the day before so the flavours develop. Be sure to remove the bay leaf before serving.

Sweet and Spicy Panko Crusted Chicken

1 cup panko
¼ cup sugar
1 tsp garlic powder
2 tsp smoked paprika
1 tsp onion powder
1 tsp coarse salt
1 tsp chili powder
Black pepper
¼ cup flour
2 eggs
2 large chicken breasts, sliced into fillets

Place flour in a shallow bowl (or on a piece of waxed paper). Beat eggs in a shallow bowl. Mix remaining ingredients and place on sheet of waxed paper. Dip chicken in flour, tossing well to coast, dip in egg, then in panko mixture. Spray baking sheet with oil, or line with parchment paper or non-stick foil. Bake at 425°F for 10 minutes per side, turning halfway through.

Layered Chicken Salad

I love this recipe and it is so great to make in the summer time — make it and refrigerate until serving. The water chestnuts are optional but make a great crunch.

SALAD
- 4 to 5 cups shredded lettuce
- ¼ lb (113 g) bean sprouts, washed well and dried
- 8 oz (236 ml) water chestnuts, sliced
- 1 English cucumber, thinly sliced
- ½ cup chopped green onion
- 8 oz (226 g) snow peas, steamed, drained and cooled (pat dry with paper towels)

DRESSING
- 2 cups mayonnaise
- 2 tsp curry powder
- ½ tsp ground ginger
- 1 tbsp lemon juice or vinegar
- Cherry tomatoes for garnish

Layer ingredients in order listed. Mix dressing ingredients and pour over, sealing to the edge. Cover with plastic wrap and refrigerate several hours. Garnish with cherry tomatoes at serving time.

Chicken Noodle Supreme

10 oz (284 g) broad noodles
1 (10 oz) (284 ml) can mushroom soup
1 (10 oz) (284 ml) can chicken soup
2 cups cooked chicken
½ cups olives
2 cups sautéed mushrooms
½ cup white wine
1 lb (454 g) cheese, grated

Cook and drain noodles, set aside. Mix remaining ingredients except cheese. Spoon mixture into a 9 by 13 inch dish that has been sprayed with cooking spray. Top with cheese. Bake at 350°F for 25 to 30 minutes or until cheese is melted and bubbly.

Chicken Tetrazinni

6 oz (170 g) spaghetti or noodles, cooked and drained
¼ cup butter
½ cup flour
2 cups chicken stock
1 cup light cream
¼ cup chopped onion
Salt
Pepper
1 cup sliced mushrooms, sautéed in a small amount of butter
2 cups chicken
Parmesan cheese

Place noodles in a 9 by 13 inch pan that has been sprayed with cooking spray. Place turkey or chicken over top. Make sauce by melting butter, then adding flour and cooking for 2 minutes. Add chicken stock and stir until thickened. Stir in cream and add mushrooms. Pour over the noodle/chicken mixture. Top with grated parmesan. Bake at 375°F for 20 minutes or until browned and bubbly.

This is always one of my go-to recipes for leftover turkey. It freezes very well.

Bengal Curry

2 lb (1 kg) chicken pieces
1 to 2 cups chicken broth

Parboil chicken for 15 minutes. Remove chicken from pan and remove bones. Set aside.

CURRY SAUCE

¼ cup butter
2 medium onions, chopped
1 clove garlic, minced
2 tbsp curry powder
½ cup ketchup
2 tbsp milk
Reserved chicken broth, fat skimmed off
¼ cup raisins
4 chopped apples, peeled
1 to 2 tbsp flour
1 cup chopped green pepper

Melt butter and sauté onions and garlic. Add curry powder. Cook until fragrant. Add remaining ingredients, including chicken. Simmer 40 to 60 minutes or until apples and peppers are tender. Serve with hot cooked rice.

Easy Chicken Divan

1 bunch fresh broccoli, tough stems removed, cut into bite size pieces and steamed lightly
2 cups sliced cooked chicken
2 10 oz cans cream of chicken soup
1 cup mayonnaise
1 tsp lemon juice
1 tsp curry powder
½ cup soft bread crumbs
1 tsp butter or margarine

Place broccoli in baking dish. Top with slices or chunks of chicken. Mix soup, mayonnaise, lemon juice and curry powder together and pour over chicken and broccoli. Mix soft breadcrumbs with butter and use to top casserole. Bake 25 to 30 minutes in a 325°F oven.

Fruity Chicken Salad

DRESSING
4 tbsp orange juice
5 tbsp low-fat mayonnaise
3 tbsp low-fat sour cream
1 tsp brown sugar and vinegar
½ tsp curry powder

SALAD
1 lb (454 g) shredded chicken
½ lb (227 g) green or red grapes, cut in half
Salt
Pepper
Large ripe avocado, cut into chunks
Toasted pine nuts and drained mandarin oranges for garnish

Mix all together and serve on a bed of lettuce. Garnish with toasted pine nuts and drained mandarin oranges.

Chicken Enchiladas

TORTILLAS

1 cup flour
½ cup cornmeal
½ tsp salt

1 egg
1½ cups cold water

Combine ingredients and beat until smooth. Spoon 3 tablespoons onto lightly oiled pan to make a 6-inch tortilla. Turn when edges start to look dry. Keep warm until all are cooked.

ENCHILADA SAUCE

3 tbsp finely chopped onion
2 tbsp oil
2 tbsp flour
1 (19 oz) (560 ml) can diced tomatoes, undrained

1 clove garlic, minced
1 tbsp chili powder
1 tsp salt
Tabasco sauce, as desired
2 or 3 chopped jalapeno peppers

Brown onion in oil, stir in remaining ingredients. Simmer 30 to 40 minutes. If you prefer a chunky sauce, use as is. If you prefer a smoother sauce, purée sauce with immersion blender.

FILLING

2 or 3 chicken breasts, poached or use leftover chicken or turkey
Salt

2½ cups shredded cheddar cheese
¾ cup sour cream

Cut chicken into strips. Sprinkle with salt. On each tortilla, spread a spoonful of sauce, top with chicken, then cheese. Roll up and place in lightly oiled 9 by 13 inch pan. Continue until all are used. To remaining sauce, add sour cream. Pour over enchiladas and top with remaining cheese. Bake at 350°F for 30 to 45 minutes until bubbly and brown.

This is another dish I always make after having turkey. My daughter can't handle corn, so we usually use flour tortillas for her portion. If you're in a hurry, the ready prepared tortillas are an option but these tortillas are more like crêpes, they are so much more tender than the prepared tortillas.

Jalapeno Stuffed Chicken Breasts

½ cup chopped canned jalapeno peppers
8 oz (226 g) cream cheese, at room temperature

4 bone-in, skin on, chicken breasts
Salt
Pepper

Mix jalapeno peppers and cream cheese. Spread mixture under skin of chicken. Season with salt and pepper. Bake on parchment paper-lined baking sheet at 400°F until cooked through, 30 to 35 minutes. Crisp skin under broiler if desired.

> *We also raised pigs, chickens and cattle on our small farm. My father warned us that we could not give names to the livestock (except for the milk cows) because any one of them could easily be Sunday dinner.*

Tangy Chicken With Pilaf

1 tbsp plus 1 tsp vegetable oil
4 chicken leg quarters plus 3 bone-in chicken breasts (or whole cut-up chicken)
1 large onion, chopped

3 cloves garlic, chopped
4 plum tomatoes, chopped
¾ cup cider vinegar
2 medium carrots, diced
1½ cups orzo or rice

Preheat oven to 400°F. In a large Dutch oven or heavy pot, heat 1 tablespoon of oil over high heat. Season chicken with salt and pepper. In batches, brown chicken, skin side first until golden and crisp, about 7 minutes. Transfer to plate. Pour off all but 1 tablespoon of fat from pan and reduce heat to medium high. Add onions and cook until transparent. Add garlic and cook until just fragrant. Add tomatoes, season with salt and pepper and cook until tomatoes start to break down, about 3 minutes. Stir in vinegar. Return chicken to pot and cook, uncovered, about 30 minutes until chicken is cooked through. Meanwhile, heat the 1 teaspoon of oil in a pan. Add carrots and cook until slightly softened. Add rice or orzo and 1¾ cups water and bring to a boil. Lower heat and cover. Cook until water is absorbed and orzo is tender, about 15 minutes. Remove from heat, fluff with fork. Serve with chicken pieces.

Chicken Lasagne

2 cups chopped cooked chicken
2 cups mushrooms, sliced
2 tbsp butter
1 cup diced onion
1 pkg (85 g) hollandaise sauce
Basil
Oregano
½ box oven ready lasagne noodles
1 cup shredded mozzarella
½ cup shredded parmesan

Sauté mushrooms and onions in butter until translucent. Set aside. Prepare sauce according to package directions. Layer, in greased 9 by 13 inch pan, ¼ of the sauce, noodles, chicken, onions, mushrooms, sprinkled with basil and oregano. Repeat, ending with remaining sauce. Add ½ cup boiling water around edges. Top with mozzarella, then parmesan. Bake at 350°F for 30 to 40 minutes. Let stand 10 minutes before cutting.

Pineapple Chicken

2 large chicken breasts

BATTER

1 egg
⅔ cup milk
1 tbsp oil

1 cup flour
1½ tsp baking powder
1 tsp salt

Mix all ingredients, let stand 10 minutes. Slice 2 large chicken breasts into 2-inch squares. Mix into batter. Heat oil 1 inch deep in skillet. Deep fry until golden, turning once. Drain on paper towels.

PINEAPPLE SAUCE

1 cup water
Dash salt
¼ cup white sugar
¼ cup brown sugar
1 tbsp vinegar

¼ cup water with 2 tbsp cornstarch
⅔ cup pineapple juice with tidbits

Cook together, water, salt, sugars, vinegar and pineapple juice. Bring to a boil. Stir in cornstarch mixture and cook until thick. Add pineapple. Serve with chicken balls.

When I was 13, I spent the entire summer at a logging camp in Caribou Country. The camp had limited electricity: a generator used only for necessary refrigeration. We were so far north, there was little need for electricity for lighting, the summer daylight is nearly 18 hours long. We cooked with a wood stove and a smoker. We cooked dishes in big batches that could do for several meals. My sister-in-law, who also worked at the camp, did the shopping and bought enough to last for two weeks at a time. Then we would cook a huge ham or turkey. The meat would be used for sandwiches for the loggers' lunches and a lot of other meals.

Ginger Glazed Pork Tenderloin

¼ cup sliced green onion
2 cloves garlic, minced
¼ tsp salt
2 tbsp soy sauce
½ tsp pepper

2 tbsp honey
2 pork tenderloins,
   silver skin removed
1 tbsp molasses

Mix sauce ingredients. Marinate tenderloins at least 30 minutes. Drain off marinade into a small saucepan, bring to a boil and boil 2 minutes. BBQ or broil tenderloin, brushing with glaze often. Always boil the glaze for the recommended time to eliminate any bacteria from the meat that may be in the marinade.

When I buy pork tenderloin it usually comes in packages of two. I peel the silver skin off each tenderloin, then cut off the small ends and put them into a separate container. I pound the ends with a meat mallet until they are about a quarter inch thick and use them for schnitzel. You can make a marinade for the centre tenderloin, then place it along with the marinade in a freezer bag and freeze it. When you thaw it, it will already be marinated.

Teriyaki Pork Chops

4 pork chops, ½-inch thick
1 tbsp oil
½ cup chicken stock
1 tbsp grated fresh ginger
2 cloves garlic, crushed

⅓ cup slivered almonds
2 tsp cornstarch
⅓ cup teriyaki sauce
2 cups snow peas
1 green onion, sliced

Brown chops well in oil. Remove from pan. Brown almonds and set aside. Blend chicken stock, ginger, garlic, teriyaki sauce and cornstarch. Add to pan and cook to thicken. Return chops to pan, top with snow peas and cover. Simmer 5 to 10 minutes, until chops are cooked.

Dr. Pepper Pulled Pork

For this recipe, I can't stress enough that you buy a shoulder. A loin has no fat and cooking it for long periods of time makes it tough. When you pull the pork, discard any fat.

- 3 to 4 lb pork shoulder
- 24 oz (2 cans) Dr. Pepper or any soda with spices and sugar (not diet)
- 1 medium onion, diced
- 1½ tsp dry mustard
- 2 cloves garlic, crushed
- ¼ tsp cayenne
- Salt
- Pepper
- ¼ cup cider vinegar
- 3 tbsp Worcestershire sauce
- BBQ sauce

Put onion in a slow cooker, place pork on top. Add all other ingredients except BBQ sauce. Pour Dr. Pepper over. Cook on low 8 hours or on high 3 to 4 hours. Carefully remove meat and let cool on a plate until cool enough to handle. With two forks, shred meat, discarding all fat. Return to slow cooker and simmer for 2 hours. Drain remaining juices and mix meat with enough BBQ sauce to moisten to desired sauciness. Serve in warmed buns with coleslaw.

Tortière

¾ lb (340) ground pork
2 tbsp finely chopped onion
1 clove garlic, minced
¾ tsp salt
Black pepper
¼ tsp celery salt
⅛ tsp sage
Pinch cloves
1 large potato, cubed
9-inch pie shell; pie crust for top

Place all ingredients in skillet and cook until potatoes are tender and pork is no longer pink. Mash well. If any liquid is remaining, add a few dry breadcrumbs to soak it up. Take a prepared 9-inch pie shell. Pour pork mixture into it. Add second crust, cut vents and bake in 425°F oven for 10 minutes. Reduce heat to 350°F and bake 45 minutes longer.

Sweet and Sour Spareribs

2 racks (3 lb/1.5 kg) spareribs
Salt
Pepper
¼ cup finely chopped onion
¼ cup finely chopped celery
¼ cup diced green pepper
2 tbsp butter
1 tbsp cornstarch
1 tbsp brown sugar
1 cup unsweetened pineapple juice
¼ cup vinegar
1 tbsp soy sauce

Heat oven to 400°F. Line a shallow pan with foil. Cut ribs into serving size pieces. Sprinkle with salt and pepper. Arrange in pan and bake in hot oven for 30 minutes. Meanwhile, prepare sauce. Sauté onion, celery and green pepper in butter until tender crisp, about 5 minutes. Stir together cornstarch, sugar, pineapple juice, vinegar and soy sauce. Add to pan. Cook until thickened. Pour off excess fat from ribs. Brush on glaze and return to oven. Reduce heat to 300°F and continue to bake, stirring occasionally until well glazed, about 30 minutes. Add pineapple chunks, if desired.

Thai Salad with Pork

DRESSING

1/3 cup peanut butter
1/3 cup vegetable oil
2 tbsp lemon juice
1 clove garlic, minced
1/2 tsp red pepper flakes
1/4 tsp ground ginger
1/4 cup warm water

Purée all ingredients above in blender. Set aside.

SALAD

6 large slices leftover pork tenderloin (or sauté 6 boneless pork chops, brushing with soy sauce)
1 head lettuce
1 cup bean sprouts
1 cucumber, sliced
1 red pepper, thinly sliced
3 green onions, sliced
French fried onions, if desired

Assemble salad, top with pork. Toss with dressing and garnish with onions.

Pork and Apple Meatballs

1 tart apple, peeled and grated
¼ cup quick cooking oatmeal
¼ cup milk
1 lb (454 g) ground pork
2 cloves garlic, minced
½ tsp crumbled sage
Salt

Pepper
1 large onion, chopped
1 tsp cinnamon
½ cup apple jelly
1 red pepper, chopped
1 cup frozen shelled edamame

Working over bowl, squeeze juice from grated apple, using your hands. Add enough water to make ¼ cup. Set aside. In another bowl, place apple, oatmeal and milk. Let soak 5 minutes Add pork, garlic, sage, 1 teaspoon of salt and ¼ teaspoon of pepper. Mix lightly. Scoop mixture into meatballs. Place on foil-lined baking sheet. Bake 10 minutes at 375°F. Transfer to slow cooker. In a skillet, add 1 teaspoon of oil and sauté onion until translucent. Stir in cinnamon, apple jelly and reserved juice. Cook, stirring until jelly melts. Pour over meatballs and cook on low 6 hours, or on high for 3 hours. Stir in red pepper and edamame. Cook another 20 minutes until vegetables are tender crisp.

Garlic Spareribs

1 cup ketchup
1 cup water
1 tsp Worcestershire sauce
1 tsp chili powder
¼ cup vinegar
1 tsp paprika

¾ cup brown sugar
Salt
Pepper
2 cloves garlic, chopped
3 lb (1.5 kg) spareribs

Cut spareribs into serving size pieces. Roast in a 400°F oven for 45 minutes. While spareribs are cooking, simmer all other ingredients together. When ribs are cooked, pour off all fat. Pour sauce over, turning to coat all sides. Cover and return to oven. Reduce heat to 300°F for 45 minutes to 1 hour. Remove cover for last 30 minutes of cooking. Can be placed in slow cooker after browning period and cooked 4 to 5 hours on low.

Maple Glazed Pork Medallions

1 lb (454 g) pork tenderloin, cut into twelve half-inch slices
1½ tsp fresh thyme or ½ tsp dried
½ tsp coarse salt
2 tbsp maple syrup
1 tbsp Dijon mustard
2 tsp extra virgin olive oil

¾ cup fresh orange juice
2½ by ½ inch strip of orange peel cut into long, thin strips
1 clove garlic, minced
Salt
Pepper

Sprinkle pork with thyme, salt and pepper. Combine maple syrup and mustard in a small cup. Pound pork between sheets of waxed paper or plastic wrap to ¼ inch. Heat large skillet over medium high heat until hot. Cook pork 2 to 4 minutes, until lightly browned, turning once. Remove pork, add orange juice, orange rind and garlic to skillet and boil 2 to 3 minutes until reduced by half. Stir in maple syrup mixture. Add pork and stir until pork is glazed. Remove orange peel.

Pomegranate Glazed Pork Medallions

SAUCE

1 tsp butter
1 large shallot, minced
1 clove garlic, minced
1 tsp coriander seed, crushed
1 cup pomegranate juice
¼ cup ruby port

MEDALLIONS

2 pork tenderloins, cut in 1½-inch slices
2 tbsp butter
2 tbsp olive oil
¼ cup flour
½ tsp salt
Black pepper
½ cup chicken broth
1 small pomegranate seeded (or use pomegranate arils prepared in store)

Melt butter. Add shallot and coriander seed. Sauté 1 minute or until fragrant. Add juice and port. Increase heat to medium high and cook until reduced by half. Remove from heat and set aside.

Remove silver skin from outside of pork. Slice and place between sheets of waxed paper or plastic wrap. Pound, with meat mallet or rolling pin, to ½-inch thickness. Melt butter and olive oil in skillet. Place flour on piece of waxed paper. Dip pork pieces in flour and quickly sauté in oil/butter mixture. Remove to plate and keep warm. When all are cooked, add back to skillet with sauce and cook until the medallions are glazed and heated through.

Pepper Roast

3 to 4 lb (1 to 2 kg) cross rib or top sirloin roast, boned, tied and rolled
2 tbsp crushed black peppercorns
½ tsp crushed garlic
½ tsp dried oregano
2 tbsp Dijon mustard
1 tbsp lemon juice

Combine seasonings. Rub over surface of beef. Let stand 30 minutes. Cook on BBQ rotisserie 45 minutes per pound, or until meat thermometer measures medium rare. Let stand, covered in foil, 10 minutes before carving.

Stir Fry Beef and Broccoli

1 lb (454 g) thinly sliced sirloin steak
2 lb (908 g) broccoli, cut into bite-sized pieces
4 tbsp soy sauce
4 tsp cornstarch
3 tbsp sherry
2 tbsp vegetable oil
2 cloves garlic, crushed
¼ cup water
2 to 3 chunks of fresh ginger, diced

Mix together. Divide marinade in two and marinate beef and broccoli separately at least 1 hour. Drain off marinade. In wok, add 3 tablespoons of oil and heat to high. Stir fry meat for 3 to 4 minutes. Remove meat and add 1 tablespoon of oil to wok. Add broccoli. Stir 2 to 3 minutes. Add ¼ cup water and steam 3 to 4 minutes longer. Add meat and reserved marinade. Stir fry until sauce is clear and thickened. Remove pieces of ginger. Serve with hot cooked rice.

Cocoa Crusted Beef Tenderloin

This recipe was one we had on a cruise ship. I was lucky enough to be put on the cruise ship's website and they willingly shared recipes. It seems like an unlikely combination but you won't believe how good it is.

4 beef tenderloin medallions, 1½-inch thick
½ tsp salt
¼ tsp black pepper
3 tbsp unsweetened cocoa powder
3 tbsp finely ground coffee

Preheat broiler or grill. Sprinkle steaks with salt and pepper. In a spice grinder, finely grind coffee and cocoa. Spread mixture on sheet of waxed paper. Dip steaks in coffee and cocoa mixture and shake off excess. Place on broiler. Broil 3 to 4 inches from heat source, for 9 to 11 minutes on each side, or until the meat is done to your liking.

Boeuf Bourguignon

BEEF

6 slices bacon, cooked and crumbled
4 lb (1.5 kg) beef sirloin, cut into cubes or strips
2 tbsp brandy
2 lb sliced mushrooms
1 cup diced onion
3 to 4 carrots, sliced
Seasoned flour

Toss beef in seasoned flour. In bacon drippings, sear meat in batches until all is cooked. Place in ovenproof casserole. Warm brandy. Pour over beef and ignite. In the same skillet, add small amount of butter if necessary and sauté mushrooms until liquid evaporates. Add to casserole. Sauté onions and add to casserole along with carrots.

BOURGUIGNON SAUCE

3 cups beef broth
1½ cups dry red wine
2 bay leaves
2 tbsp chopped parsley
1 tsp each salt and thyme
⅛ tsp pepper

Add all sauce ingredients to casserole with beef. Cover and simmer 1½ to 2 hours in 300°F oven. To thicken, blend together 3 tablespoons of butter and 1 cup of flour. Add to dish, one tablespoonful at a time, until desired thickness is reached. Serve with crusty bread and/or mashed potatoes.

Teriyaki Smoked Pork Loin

⅔ cup soy sauce
2 tsp dry mustard
¼ cup cooking oil
2 tsp ground ginger
2 tbsp molasses
2 cloves garlic, chopped
Rolled pork loin roast

Combine all ingredients, except pork. Set aside. Insert spit through centre of roast. Cook 3 hours on a barbecue rotisserie over medium heat, brushing with soy sauce mixture after first hour.

Cabbage Rolls

This is a recipe that has been in my family for generations. My lone contribution to this recipe was quite by accident. When I returned from grocery shopping one day, I asked one of my kids to toss the bag with the meat into the freezer. Unbeknownst to me, there was a head of cabbage in the same bag. Several days later when I wanted to make cabbage rolls I could not find the cabbage. When I did discover it in the freezer, I let it thaw and lo and behold, it was as pliable as if it had been steamed with no extra work involved. The cabbage must be solidly frozen (left in the freezer for 2 to 3 days) and then thawed either in the sink or in a bucket. When you go to use it, just cut the core out and pull off the leaves, then remove the hard vein from each leaf before using.

1 lb (454 g) lean ground beef
2 to 2½ cups cooked rice
4 slices bacon, diced, uncooked
1 large onion, finely diced
2 cloves garlic, minced
Salt
Pepper
14 oz (414 ml) can diced tomatoes
10 oz (300 ml) can tomato soup
1 head of cabbage, frozen and thawed (alternatively, cabbage can be steamed until pliable)

Mix all ingredients, except cabbage, together lightly. Lay out a cabbage leaf and put a heaping tablespoonful of the ground beef mixture on it. Tuck in ends and roll up. Lay into a deep casserole and repeat until all are wrapped. Take can of diced tomatoes and mix with tomato soup. Pour over the cabbage rolls. Cover and bake at 350°F for 3 to 4 hours. Make sure you place your casserole on a deep cookie sheet as it tends to boil over. This recipe makes a lot but don't worry about wasted leftovers: they taste even better reheated the next day.

Hungarian Goulash à la Joan

2 lb (1 kg) stewing meat, fat and gristle removed
Seasoned flour
1 pkg (35 g) onion soup mix
1 (6 oz) (156 ml) can tomato paste
2½ cups water

Toss meat with seasoned flour until well coated. Brown the meat in a skillet in small amount of vegetable oil. At this point, I use my pressure cooker, but you can also braise it in the oven. For the pressure cooker, after you have browned the meat, pour in ½ cup of the water to deglaze the pan. Add all to pressure cooker, along with remaining ingredients. Put lid on, seal and add the pressure control. Bring to pressure and reduce heat and cook 10 minutes. Let cool on its own.

For oven braising, after deglazing pan, add all ingredients to casserole. Tightly cover and cook at 275°F for about 2 hours, checking occasionally and adding water as needed. Serve with spaetzle or noodles.

This recipe is also easily adapted to a slow cooker. Simply brown the meat, add to cooker, then mix the sauce over and cook on low about 8 hours.

Spaetzle

2½ cups flour
1 cup water
2 eggs
1 tbsp oil
1 tsp salt

Mix flour, eggs and salt. Add water a little at a time, beating until light and fluffy. Add oil to boiling water or chicken broth. Drop spaetzle into boiling water by using a spaetzle maker or pushing batter through the wide holes of a strainer or grater. Cook until spaetzle comes to top. Remove from broth and continue to cook a few at a time until all are done. Toss with butter. Keep warm and serve with the goulash.

Steak with Peppercorn Cream Sauce

We have long time friends in Ottawa – he loves to cook. So when we visit, my husband and his wife visit while Sam and I cook. This recipe is one he discovered and of course improved upon. It is so rich, but so good.

4 (6 oz) (170 g) filet mignon, 1½- to 2-inches thick
2 tbsp crushed black peppercorns
2 tbsp crushed white peppercorns
Salt
4 tbsp canola oil
3 tbsp brandy
¼ cup undiluted consommé
¼ cup whipping cream
3 tbsp butter
½ tsp each pink and green peppercorns

Season steaks with black and white peppercorns and salt on both sides. Heat oil in heavy pan. Sauté steaks on both sides for medium rare. Warm brandy, pour over steaks and flambé. Transfer steak to plate to keep warm. Discard fat in pan. Add stock and reduce to half. Add cream and reduce until sauce is thickened. Beat in butter, bit by bit. Add salt and pepper to taste. Add pink and green peppercorns to sauce. Pour sauce over steaks and serve immediately.

Impossible Taco Pie

1 lb (454 g) lean ground beef
½ cup chopped onion
1 envelope (35 g) taco seasoning
4 oz (118 ml) can chopped green chilies
¼ cup milk
¾ cup biscuit mix
3 eggs
2 tomatoes, diced
1 cup shredded cheese
Shredded lettuce

Brown ground beef and onion together. Drain off any fat. Stir in seasoning mix. Spread into greased 9-inch pie plate. Top with chilies. Beat milk, biscuit mix and eggs together until smooth. Pour into pie plate. Bake 25 minutes or until toothpick comes out clean. Top with cheese, bake 8 to 10 minutes longer. Cool 5 minutes. Garnish with chopped tomatoes, shredded lettuce and more shredded cheese.

Baked Bean Casserole

½ lb (250 g) bacon
½ lb (250 g) ground beef
¼ cup brown sugar
½ cup chopped celery
½ cup chopped onion
½ cup ketchup
½ cup chopped green pepper
1 tsp dry mustard
2 tbsp vinegar
1 (8 oz) (398 ml) can tomato sauce
1 cup sliced mushrooms, sautéed in small amount of butter
2 (14 oz) (414 ml) cans pork and beans
1 (14 oz) (414 ml) can kidney beans

In a large skillet, brown bacon and ground beef with onions, celery and green pepper. Drain off any fat. Pour into a greased casserole dish. Bake at 350°F for 25 to 30 minutes.

This is a super recipe for a potluck. Makes a huge amount but keeps several days in the fridge.

Sausage Strata

This is one of my favourite go-to brunch recipes – especially nice for Christmas morning because it can be put together the day before and baked while the presents are being opened. I have also made it up, frozen it and let it thaw in the fridge overnight before baking.

8 slices French bread or Italian bread, cut into cubes, crust removed
2 lb (1 kg) bulk pork sausage
¾ lb (340 g) grated old cheddar cheese
6 eggs, beaten
2½ cups whole milk
1 (10 oz) (284 ml) can cream of mushroom soup

Lay bread in bottom of greased 9 by 13 inch casserole. Alternate layers of cooked, crumbled sausage and cheese over the bread. Beat eggs with milk, pour over the layers in the casserole. Refrigerate overnight, tightly covered. In the morning, preheat oven to 325°F. Top casserole with undiluted soup. Bake 1½ hours.

Asian Meatballs

1½ lb (700 g) lean ground beef
¼ cup soft bread crumbs
1 egg
1 tsp grated fresh ginger
Salt
Pepper
¼ cup hoisin sauce
3 tbsp minced green onion
2 cloves chopped garlic
1 tsp sesame oil

Line a cookie sheet with parchment paper. Preheat oven to 400°F. Combine ingredients lightly by hand. Form into 1-inch balls with damp hands. Place on prepared baking sheet. Bake 15 to 18 minutes and set aside to keep warm while you prepare the sauce.

SAUCE
1 cup coconut milk
2 tbsp soy sauce
2 tbsp chopped fresh basil
1 tsp grated lemon zest
⅓ cup hoisin sauce
2 tbsp peanut butter
1 tbsp grated ginger
Crushed red pepper flakes,
   to taste

Whisk all ingredients together. Heat until sauce boils. Add meatballs and mix well. Cook until heated through. This recipe can be made using frozen meatballs – you won't get the flavours from the Asian spices, but they are still good if you're in a hurry.

Five Minute Stir Fry

⅔ lb (340 g) frozen shrimp
2 cups snow peas
1 red pepper, thinly sliced
½ cup teriyaki sauce
1 green pepper, thinly sliced
2 cups baby spinach

Defrost shrimp and peel. Remove strings from snow peas. Lightly coat pan with oil and heat. When pan is hot, add shrimp. Cook until they turn pink, about 2 minutes. Add peppers, peas and sauce. Stir fry until tender crisp, 3 to 4 minutes. Stir in spinach. Remove from heat, cover and let stand a few minutes until spinach wilts. Serve with rice or rice stick noodles.

Eggs in Baskets

FOR EACH SERVING

2 to 3 thin slices black forest ham
1 egg (2 if using large muffin cups or custard cups)
1 tbsp cream
Sprinkle of fresh basil
1 tbsp grated Swiss cheese
English muffins, cut in half

Grease muffin cups or ramekins. Line ramekins with ham. Break egg or eggs over. Sprinkle with cheese and basil. Bake 12 to 15 min in 350°F oven. Serve over toasted English muffin halves.

Pecan Crusted Salmon

1 cup chopped toasted pecans
1 tsp paprika
2 cloves garlic, minced
2 (8 oz) (225 g) salmon fillets
Salt
Pepper
Butter, as needed

Toast pecans in dry skillet until fragrant. Finely chop. Mix with garlic, paprika, salt and pepper. Melt some butter and brush each salmon fillet on both sides. Coat both sides of salmon with pecan mixture. Melt 2 tablespoons of butter over medium high heat. Cook about 4 minutes on each side, watching carefully not to burn. Transfer to a 350°F oven and bake for about 8 minutes.

Christmas Morning Breakfast Casserole

16 slices whole grain bread, crusts removed	1 tsp dry mustard
Sliced ham	¼ cup minced onion
Sliced old cheese	¼ cup chopped green pepper
6 eggs	2 tsp Worcestershire sauce
Salt	3 cups milk
Pepper	½ cup melted butter
	Cornflake crumbs

In a greased 9 by 13 inch casserole, layer 8 slices of bread, adding enough bread pieces to completely cover the bottom of the dish. Cover bread layer with ham slices, then cheese slices. Cover ham and cheese layer with remaining bread. Beat together eggs, milk, mustard, onion, salt, pepper, green pepper and Worcestershire sauce. Cover and let stand in fridge overnight. In the morning, melt butter and sprinkle over top. Top with cornflake crumbs and bake at 350°F for an 1 hour or more, until top is browned and egg mixture is firm. Let stand 10 minutes before serving.

Creamy Fettuccine Primavera

¾ cup milk
½ cup low-fat mayonnaise
½ tsp basil

Mix together and set aside:

Cook 2 to 4 servings of fettuccine until al dente.

1 medium carrot, julienned
1 small zucchini, julienned
½ cup red pepper, julienned

OR

3 cups julienned vegetables of your choice, i.e. mushrooms, broccoli, etc.

2 tbsp butter
½ cup grated parmesan cheese
Salt
Pepper

In a skillet, cook vegetables in butter until just tender crisp. Add milk and mayo mixture and cook until hot. Season with salt and pepper. Toss with fettuccine and cheese.

Antipasto Salad

DRESSING

¼ cup extra virgin olive oil
¼ cup cider vinegar
2 tbsp fresh lemon juice
2 tbsp fresh oregano
1 clove garlic, minced
Salt and Pepper

SALAD

1 (20 oz) (700 g) pkg cheese tortellini
1 (14 oz) (414 ml) can artichoke hearts, drained
1 cup grape tomatoes
1 cup sliced pepperoni
1 cup diced fresh mozzarella
½ cup kalamata olives
Fresh basil

Cook tortellini according to package directions. Drain and rinse until cool. Whisk dressing ingredients together, toss with cooled tortellini and remaining ingredients. Garnish with fresh basil. This dish is best if made several hours before serving.

Philly Cheesesteak Subs

STEAK SEASONING

1 tbsp creamy horseradish
1 tbsp Dijon mustard
1 tsp Italian dressing
2 lb top sirloin or flank steak 1-inch thick

VEGETABLES

2 onions, sliced
1 large green pepper, sliced
2 tsp olive oil

Position broiler four inches below heat source. Preheat. Combine steak seasoning, horseradish, mustard and dressing. Rub seasoning mixture over meat. Broil meat, turning once, 8 to 10 minutes for medium rare. Let stand, tented with foil, while you prepare remaining ingredients.

Sauté onions and peppers in olive oil until softened but not mushy. Open sub rolls, place cheese slice on bottom of bun (or cheese sauce, if preferred) top with thinly sliced steak and vegetable mixture.

Grilled Prosciutto Sandwiches with Onion Jam

JAM

2 large sweet onions, sliced
1 cup dry red wine
1 tbsp honey
1 tbsp red wine vinegar
¼ tsp crushed red pepper flakes
Salt
Pepper
4 tsp apricot preserves

Place onion and wine in skillet. Bring to boil. Reduce heat, cover and simmer 30 minutes. Stir in honey, vinegar, pepper flakes, salt and pepper. Simmer another 30 minutes or until liquid is evaporated. Stir in apricot preserves and continue to cook 3 to 5 minutes or until onions are glazed. Cool slightly.

SANDWICHES

4 slices cinnamon raisin bread
8 thin slices prosciutto or deli ham
4 slices aged cheddar
3 tbsp soft butter

Spread 4 slices bread evenly with onion jam. Layer with prosciutto and cheese. Top with remaining bread. Butter outside of sandwich. Grill in panini press or skillet until golden brown.

Shrimp Remoulade

⅓ cup extra virgin olive oil
4 tsp Creole mustard (or grainy Dijon)
1 tsp salt
¼ cup finely chopped onion
½ tsp pepper
1 cup chopped celery
1 tsp horseradish
1 tbsp chopped parsley
2 tbsp vinegar
Cooked shrimp

Blend all ingredients together for 1 minute, until finely chopped. Chill. Just before serving, arrange cooked shrimp on a bed of lettuce. Pour sauce over.

This is a great substitute for shrimp cocktail. It's glamorous and easy to make.

Mandarin Shrimp Crêpes

BASIC CRÊPES

3 eggs	1 cup flour
1½ cups milk	½ tsp salt
3 tbsp melted butter	

Combine all ingredients in a blender until smooth. Let stand 30 minutes or more. Pour ¼ cup or less of batter in lightly oiled skillet. Cook until bubbles just start to form. Turn and cook 30 seconds more. Remove to plate and keep warm until all are cooked.

FILLING

½ lb (225 g) uncooked shrimp, shelled	1 tbsp grated fresh ginger
	1 clove garlic, minced
2 tbsp oil	2 cups snow peas, strings removed
2 tbsp sliced green onions	

In a skillet, sauté shrimp in oil for a few minutes, until shrimp just start to turn pink. Add onions, ginger, garlic and snow peas. Toss and cook 1 to 2 minutes. Fill crêpes and arrange in baking dish.

SAUCE

2 tbsp cornstarch	1 cup chicken broth
1 tbsp lemon juice	1 (10 oz) (284 ml) can mandarin oranges
1 tbsp sugar	
2 tbsp soy sauce	

Combine cornstarch, lemon juice, sugar, soy sauce and chicken broth. Cook, stirring, until thick. Add oranges. Spoon over crêpes. Heat in oven at 350°F for 10 to 12 minutes.

Once we had established ourselves here in Kingston-Greenwood, we got into the habit of inviting friends over every year for Christmas brunch. These events would include anywhere from six to 15 people. One of our young friends was "Patrick". Patrick adored my sausage strata. Now, after close to 20 years, he can't see me without asking for that dish. He says his mom makes my recipe, but it's still not like Joan's and he was very disappointed when his mom made bacon and eggs for brunch this past Christmas.

Seafood Casserole

This recipe was from the original Cy's Seafood Restaurant in Moncton. We liked it very much and I was delighted when they divulged the recipe to me. The recipe makes a large amount, can feed 12 easily but you can cut it down to feed 4 to 6.

2 cups chopped onion
3 cups chopped celery
3 tbsp butter
1 tsp salt
Dash pepper
5 cups whole milk
¾ cup flour
½ cup butter
1 lb (454 g) grated cheese

10 oz (284 g) lobster, cut in bite size pieces
½ lb (250 g) crab meat, cartilage picked out, cut into bite size pieces
¾ lb (340 g) shrimp
1 lb (454 g) scallops, cut in quarters

In a skillet, sauté celery and onion in first amount of butter. Add salt and pepper. In a saucepan, bring milk to boil. Mix flour with butter and add to milk along with celery and onions. Cook until thick. Add cheese and cook until melted. Add seafood and place entire mixture in large casserole or individual ones. Heat at 350°F in oven until bubbling and browned.

Salmon with Lemon Rice Dressing

2 salmon fillets
3 tbsp butter
⅓ cup chopped onion
1 cup diced celery
3 cups cooked rice

1 tbsp lemon rind
½ tsp salt
¼ tsp thyme
¼ cup lemon juice

Place one piece of salmon on non-stick foil. Cook butter, onion and celery together until tender. Have cooked rice, lemon rind, salt, thyme and lemon juice ready in a separate bowl and add onion and celery to the rice. Place one piece of salmon on non-stick foil, put rice over. Add second piece of salmon. Tie salmon pieces with string to encase stuffing. Wrap foil around and BBQ until fish flakes easily, or cook in 425°F oven for about 15 minutes or 10 minutes per inch of thickness.

Stuffed Salmon

2 salmon fillets, cleaned and patted dry with paper towel

DRESSING

1 (300-g) can lobster or shrimp
5 cups soft breadcrumbs
1 cup chopped celery
3 tbsp finely chopped onion
1 tbsp lemon juice
1 tbsp lemon zest
2 tbsp chopped parsley
1 tsp salt
¼ tsp pepper
⅓ cup melted butter
½ cup white wine

Preheat oven to 450°F. Butter a sheet of foil large enough to wrap around the salmon (or use non-stick foil). Place one piece of salmon on foil. Cover with dressing. Place second fillet over top. Fold foil over fish and seal into a packet. Place on baking sheet and bake at 450°F for 10 minutes per inch of thickness, or until fish flakes easily with a fork.

I grew up in British Columbia and our household was dirt poor. We learned to live off what we could grow or catch. Our village had the Shuswap River running through it — a river where four of the five species of Pacific salmon spawn. The two of my older brothers who were still at home when I was a child were avid fishermen. In the fall, we would have salmon frequently. The largest fish either of my brothers ever brought home weighed 36 pounds. My brother was only about 14 years old at the time and the fish was bigger than he was! Although it wasn't a particularly good fish to eat, the photos were quite impressive. Most of the fish were much smaller than that whopper, at 8 to 10 pounds. My mom would can all the fish that we couldn't eat fresh and we would have salmon all year long.

Shrimp with Salsa Crude

4 large ripe tomatoes, peeled, seeded and chopped
2 hot peppers
1 tsp salt
1 cup chopped onion
¼ tsp pepper
¼ cup chopped cilantro
1 tbsp sugar
½ cup chopped celery
½ cup chopped green pepper
2 tbsp red wine vinegar
1 tsp mustard seed
1 tbsp olive oil
Tabasco sauce, if desired
½ lb frozen cooked shrimp, shells removed
8 oz (225 g) spaghetti or linguini

Seed the hot peppers and chop finely. Place in a bowl and add remaining ingredients. Let stand 30 minutes to develop flavours. Cook spaghetti or linguini until al dente in boiling, salted water. Add frozen cooked shrimp to boiling pasta for last minute. Drain and toss with some of the salsa until at desired taste.

Garlic and Shrimp with White Beans

1 lb (454 g) medium shrimp, peeled and deveined
4 tbsp olive oil, divided
1 tsp smoked paprika
3 cloves garlic, minced and divided
½ tsp hot pepper sauce
1 bay leaf
14 oz (414 ml) can diced tomatoes, drained
1 tbsp tomato paste
2 (15 oz) (450 ml) cans white beans, drained and rinsed
1 cup chicken broth
3 tbsp chopped fresh parsley

Heat a skillet over medium high heat. Toss shrimp with 1 tablespoon of oil and paprika. Sauté for 1 to 2 minutes and add half the garlic. Sauté 30 seconds more. Place shrimp in a bowl. Return skillet to heat. Add 2 tablespoons of oil, pepper flakes, bay leaf and remaining garlic. Add tomatoes and cook until most of the moisture has evaporated. Add tomato paste and cook until mixture darkens. Add beans and broth and simmer until thick. Stir in shrimp and parsley. Drizzle with remaining oil.

Seafood and Spinach Casserole

2 small haddock fillets
½ lb (225 g) crabmeat, discard any shell and cartilage
½ lb (225 g) fresh scallops, halved
Meat from 2 lobsters, roughly chopped or use 1 300-g can lobster, drained and chopped
1 cup buttered bread crumbs

BECHAMEL SAUCE

2 tbsp butter
2 tbsp flour
2 cups milk
Pinch nutmeg
Salt
Pepper

Melt butter, whisk in flour, cook a few minutes. Add heated milk and cook until thickened. Season to taste.

SPINACH LAYER

2 (285 g) pkgs frozen chopped spinach, thawed and squeezed dry
1 tbsp butter
1 rib celery, diced
1 clove garlic, minced
¼ cup finely chopped onion
1 red pepper, finely diced
¼ tsp thyme
2 tbsp sherry or chicken broth

Melt butter in large skillet, add spinach and cook until heated through. Add remaining ingredients.

Lay spinach mixture in buttered 9 by 13 inch pan. Top with seafood. Pour béchamel sauce over. Sprinkle with buttered bread crumbs. Bake 40 to 45 minutes at 350°F until flavours are combined.

Several years ago, I was in the hospital and the doctor came in to see me. He asked how everything was. I replied, "The food stinks, the only thing edible is the vegetable beef soup." He replied, "I should hope so — it comes from Campbell's in a bucket." The next day he arrived at my room and said, "My apologies — my office staff just informed me who you are and I can understand why you think hospital food stinks.

Lobster Thermidor in Phyllo Baskets

SHELLS

1 tbsp melted butter
4 sheets phyllo pastry
1 tbsp olive oil
¼ cup finely shredded parmesan cheese

Preheat oven to 400°F. Combine butter and oil. Layering in turn, spread 1 phyllo sheet lightly with butter and oil mixture. Sprinkle with parmesan. Lay another sheet on top and repeat. Top with fourth sheet, finishing with a brushing of oil mixture. Cut into 6 rectangles or squares. Push centre of each into cup of muffin tin, so each is somewhat apart. Allow edges to overflow to form decorative frill. Bake 8 to 10 minutes. Cool on rack.

RICE

1½ cups basmati rice
2½ cups water

Wash rice in sieve under cold running water. Turn rice into medium saucepan and measured water. Let stand 30 minutes. Bring to a boil over medium heat. Reduce heat and cook 15 minutes. Turn off heat. Let stand, covered, 15 minutes, then fluff with fork.

LOBSTER THERMIDOR

1 (300-g) can frozen lobster
2 tbsp butter
2 shallots, minced
1 tbsp Dijon mustard
¼ cup flour
½ tsp paprika
⅛ tsp cayenne
1 cup water
½ cup dry white wine
8 oz (225 g) button mushrooms, sliced
1 cup whipping cream
2 egg yolks
2 tbsp brandy
2 tbsp finely chopped parsley

Defrost lobster overnight. Press down can lid until liquid is drained off. Cut larger pieces of lobster into chunks. Melt butter until bubbly. Add shallots and cook 1 to 2 minutes. Stir in mustard. Mix flour with paprika and cayenne pepper and add to shallots. Cook 1 minute. Whisking briskly, incorporate water and wine into the mix. Bring to slow boil just until bubbles appear. Cook 2 minutes until thick and smooth. Stir in mushrooms and cook 3 to 4 minutes, until they release their liquid. Stir in cream, heat 1 to 2 minutes but do not boil. Add beaten egg yolks and brandy. Fill phyllo cups and garnish with parsley.

To assemble, place phyllo cup on serving plate. Place a heaping tablespoon of the rice in the bottom and pour the thermidor over.

Beef Stroganoff

1 lb (454 g) top sirloin steak, 1-inch thick, sliced into strips	1 cup beef broth
¼ cup flour	2 cups mushrooms, sliced and sautéed in small amount of butter
Salt	
Pepper	1 cup sour cream

Mix together flour, salt and pepper in plastic bag. Add steak and shake to coat each piece in flour. Do this in small batches so every side of beef gets floured. Add 1 tablespoon of oil to a hot skillet, brown meat pieces, being careful not to overcrowd pan. When all are browned, return to pan. Add beef broth and cook 10 minutes, until meat is tender. Add sautéed mushrooms to pan. If the broth is not thick enough, mix some of the reserved flour mixture (1 to 2 tablespoons) to cold water or beef broth. Add to pan, stir until thickened to your liking. Stir in sour cream. Do not let boil.

I do this in the pressure cooker, using round steak or stewing beef. Simply brown the floured meat, add the broth and cook about 7 to 8 minutes. Let cool on its own and then add the cooked mushrooms and sour cream. Serve over rice or noodles.

Cottage Pie with Vegetable Mash

1 lb (454 g) potatoes, peeled and diced
½ lb (230 g) carrots, peeled and diced
½ lb (230 g) sweet potatoes, peeled and diced
4 tbsp butter
1 lb (454 g) ground beef
5 cloves garlic, divided
1 medium onion, finely chopped
1 lb (454 g) button mushrooms, sliced
3 tbsp tomato paste
1 tbsp Worcestershire sauce
1 cup beef broth

Preheat oven to 450°F. Cook potatoes, carrots, sweet potatoes and 3 cloves of garlic. Simmer until vegetables are tender. Drain and return to pot. Mash vegetables until smooth. Add 3 tablespoons of butter and season with salt and pepper. Whip until fluffy. Finely chop 2 cloves garlic and set aside. Heat remaining 1 tablespoon of butter, add beef and brown about 5 minutes. Remove meat from pan. Add onions to drippings, cook until translucent, add mushrooms and cook until golden and moisture evaporates, about 10 minutes. Add chopped garlic and cook until fragrant. Return meat and any accumulated juices to pan. Stir in tomato paste. Cook, stirring about 2 minutes. Stir in Worcestershire sauce and beef broth. Reduce heat and simmer until liquid is slightly thickened, about 5 minutes. Season with salt and pepper. Place in casserole dish, top with the mashed vegetable mixture. Bake for 10 to 15 minutes until lightly browned and heated throughout.

My father passed away when I was 14 and naturally, my mom was distraught — she'd been married since she was 15 and had no education. We three kids that were at home tried to help her get through it, but it was rough. About six months after my father's death, my sister and her husband were in a terrible car accident. They had a three-month-old baby, so mom went out to help, leaving me alone with my two lumberjack brothers. Whatever I had learned about cooking certainly came into use. My daily routine started with packing lunches and preparing a full breakfast at 5:30 am. Then I would do what housework needed to be done at the house, be at school at 9 am, back home by 3:30 pm, and prepare a big meal for my brothers when they got home at suppertime. My sister-in-law pitched in a lot but I sure learned how much work it was to look after the loggers.

Jalapeno and Bacon Mac and Cheese

3 cups uncooked elbow macaroni
½ lb (225 g) bacon, chopped
1 jalapeno pepper, seeded and minced
1½ cups 2% milk
1 cup shredded Monterey Jack cheese
4 oz (114 g) processed cheese, cubed
1 tsp onion powder
1 tsp chili powder
½ tsp salt
½ tsp pepper
Dash hot pepper sauce
3 green onions, chopped

Cook macaroni in salted water accordingly to package directions. Drain and set aside. Cook bacon until crisp. Using slotted spoon, remove bacon to paper towels to drain. Drain all but 1 tablespoon of bacon fat. Sauté jalapeno pepper in drippings. Add milk, cheeses and spices. Cook until cheese melts. Add macaroni and place in baking dish. Stir in bacon. Bake 25 to 30 minutes to heat thoroughly. Garnish with green onion.

DESSERTS

Desserts have always been a favourite of mine to prepare. I think that as a child, it was a way to become "grown up" by making fantastic desserts. My sister-in-law was always baking and I always said I wanted to cook just like Karin. These desserts, although certainly not in the diet category, always impress. I wish they wouldn't affect our waistlines quite so much, but I do enjoy preparing them. It feels like artistry.

Death By Chocolate

1¼ lb (566 g) dark chocolate
¼ cup butter
2¼ cups whipping cream

2 tbsp cocoa
Peppermint extract or liqueur
2 egg whites

Heat cream with chocolate over hot water until chocolate melts. Cool until mixture is almost set. Whip egg whites until peaks form. Whip cooled chocolate mixture until it forms soft peaks. Fold in chocolate mixture and remaining ingredients. Pour into a loaf pan lined with parchment paper or buttered foil. Chill. Slice and place on plate with sauce.

SAUCE ANGLAISE

4 egg yolks
1 cup blend
2 cups whipping cream

1 cup white sugar
2 oz (60 ml) orange liqueur

Place all ingredients except liqueur in double boiler, beating egg yolks well first. Cook until custard coats the back of a spoon. Cool. Add liqueur.

Hawaiian Cream

2½ cups pineapple chunks
½ cup maraschino cherries, halved
2 cups miniature marshmallows
¼ cup reserved pineapple juice

1½ cups whipping cream, whipped
½ cup slivered almonds, toasted
½ cup toasted coconut

Combine all ingredients except cream, almonds and coconut. Let stand 1 hour. Fold in cream and almonds. Spoon into dessert dishes. Sprinkle with coconut.

Mocha Cheesecake

CRUST

26 chocolate wafers, crushed (or 1½ cups)	2 tbsp sugar
	¼ cup butter, melted

Blend and press into bottom and sides of a sprayed 9-inch springform pan. Chill.

FILLING

12 oz (340 g) semi-sweet chocolate chips	1 cup sugar
2 tbsp instant coffee	3 tbsp flour
2 tbsp hot water	3 eggs
3 8 oz (250 g) pkgs cream cheese	2 egg yolks
	1 cup heavy cream

Melt chocolate. Dissolve coffee in hot water. Beat cheese until smooth and add sugar gradually. Sprinkle flour over, blend thoroughly. Add eggs and yolks, one at a time. Slowly beat in chocolate mixture, then coffee, then cream. Pour into prepared pan. Bake in hot water bath at 350°F for 1 hour or until top is firm. Leave in oven with heat turned off for an additional hour. Cool completely, then refrigerate.

Chocolate Truffle Cake

1 Devil's food cake mix, prepared according to directions	1 lb (454 g) semi-sweet chocolate
1 cup finely chopped almonds, toasted	2 cups whipping cream
	¼ cup Amaretto

Bake cake in two, 9-inch round-cake pans. Cool. Heat cream in saucepan, just to boiling. Meanwhile, break up or finely chop chocolate. Add to hot cream and stir until melted. Continue stirring to make sure it is completely smooth. Blend in amaretto. Refrigerate and chill until cold but not firm. Remove from refrigerator and beat at medium speed until thick enough to spread. Do not overbeat as it will separate. Cut each cake layer in half. Fill each layer with the chocolate mixture and frost. Sprinkle almonds over top.

Frangelico Cake

BRITTLE

½ cup whole hazelnuts
1 tbsp corn syrup
½ cup sugar
1 tsp butter
½ tsp baking soda

Toast hazelnuts for 5 minutes. Turn onto a dish towel and rub to remove skins. Lightly grease a baking sheet or line with foil. In a microwave-safe dish, place sugar, corn syrup and nuts. Cook in the microwave for 4 minutes on high. Add butter and cook 1 minute more. Add soda. Stir until foaming stops, then spread on cookie sheet. When cool, crush in food processor.

CAKE

1 large angel food cake (either prepared from scratch or from a mix)
1½ tbsp plus 1 tbsp Frangelico liqueur
2 cups plus 2 tbsp whipping cream
2 tbsp icing sugar

Cut cake into 2 or 3 layers. Lay each layer on a separate plate. Mix 2 tablespoons of cream with 1 tablespoon of liqueur. Two hours before serving, drizzle cream and liqueur mixture over each cake layer. Just before serving, whip cream, beat in 1½ tablespoon of liqueur and sugar. Fill and frost cake, sprinkle with brittle.

When we were stationed in Cold Lake, Alberta, we owned a travel trailer. When the kids were done school in June, we pulled the trailer out to a nearby lake. Bob would commute to work from the trailer every day, go back to the house after work to shower, etc. and then come back out to the lake to join us. One weekend we had friends come out to go fishing. They had a toddler and at one point the mother went inside our trailer to change the baby. When she came out, she exclaimed to her husband, "You can't believe these people — they go camping with escargot dishes and crystal wine glasses!" No one told us we had to rough it! We were nice and cozy in the trailer and I hate wine out of plastic cups.

Apple Butter Pie

We made several of these for my son's wedding in Colorado. They'd not tasted butter tarts so this pie is similar.

1 unbaked, 9-inch deep-dish pie shell
3 tart, juicy apples, peeled and sliced
3 tbsp apple juice or water
¼ cup raisins

Place apples, juice and raisins in saucepan and cover. Steam until apples are barely tender, 3 to 5 minutes. Scrape apples into pie shell, spread evenly.

FILLING
⅔ cup brown sugar, packed
2 tbsp flour
¼ tsp nutmeg
¼ cup soft butter
¼ cup corn syrup
1 egg, beaten
1 tsp vanilla

Combine filling ingredients and pour over apples in pie shell. Bake at 425°F for 20 minutes. Reduce heat to 350°F and bake 25 to 30 minutes, until filling is just set. Cool before serving.

Cappuccino Mousse

1 cup cold, triple strength coffee
2 tbsp unflavoured gelatin
6 eggs, separated
1 cup icing sugar
⅓ cup Kahlua
⅓ cup sugar
3 cups whipping cream

In a saucepan, sprinkle gelatin over coffee. Allow gelatin to soften, then heat mixture gently until dissolved. In a large bowl, beat egg yolks with icing sugar until light and lemon-coloured. Transfer gelatin and coffee mixture to bowl with egg yolk mixture, beat together. Return combined egg yolk and gelatin mixtures to saucepan. Cook gently until egg yolks thicken and mixture resembles custard. Transfer to a metal bowl, beat in liqueur and cool in another bowl of ice water until mixture is at room temperature. Beat egg whites until stiff; slowly beat in sugar. Continue beating until stiff. Whip cream. Fold egg whites, then cream, into custard. Pour into individual dishes or large serving dish. Chill at least 3 hours.

GARNISH
1 cup whipping cream
2 tbsp icing sugar
3 tbsp Kahlua
Toasted sliced almonds

Beat whipping cream until stiff. Beat in icing sugar and liqueur. Beat combined ingredients until stiff. Pipe decoratively over mousse. Sprinkle with almonds.

Fudge Lover's Cake

¾ cup whole blanched almonds
3 eggs
5 squares semi-sweet chocolate, chopped
¼ cup milk

⅔ cup butter
1½ tsp vanilla
¾ cup sugar
½ tsp salt
⅔ cup flour

Separate eggs. Turn whole almonds into a blender or a food processor and grind fine. Lightly grease a 9-inch springform pan. Melt chocolate. Heat oven to 350°F. Cream butter until smooth. Gradually beat in sugar, 2 tablespoons at a time, until light and fluffy. Beat in egg yolks until light. Add melted chocolate, beating until thoroughly combined. Stir in vanilla and ½ cup ground almonds. Beat egg whites until stiff, then whisk egg whites into batter. Turn into pan and spread evenly. Bake 25 to 30 minutes or until done. Cool 10 minutes, then remove sides of pan.

ICING

5 squares semi-sweet chocolate
1 cup icing sugar
3 tbsp milk

¼ tsp almond extract
¼ cup butter

Melt chocolate with milk and butter. Add icing sugar and almond extract. Beat until smooth. Frost top and sides of cake, sprinkle with remaining ground almonds. Garnish with sliced almonds, if desired.

For everyone learning to cook remember it's a marathon, not a sprint. When I first met my husband, I wanted to impress him by making a lemon meringue pie. I had limited bake ware, so I used a tinfoil pie pan. I finished the pie and started to take it out of the oven after browning the meringue. I picked the pan up by the sides. The flimsy pan collapsed and I wore the pie. I cried — my husband laughed and ate most of the pie anyway, so it wasn't all bad. We always learn from our mistakes — never pick up a foil pan by the sides! Instead, carefully slide the pan out on its bottom.

Chocolate Peanut Butter Pie

SHELL

1¼ cup dry roasted peanuts   Pinch cloves
½ cup sugar   ¼ cup melted butter

Crush peanuts, sugar and cloves in food processor until the consistency of coarse crumbs. Pulse in butter. Press into a buttered 10-inch pan, bake at 350°F for 15 minutes. Cool.

SHELL LINING

6 oz bittersweet chocolate   ¼ cup heavy cream

Melt chocolate and cream together, Whisk together until smooth. Spread over pie crust and cool. Freeze while making filling.

FILLING

½ cup milk   Pinch salt
2 eggs   4 oz cream cheese
1 cup icing sugar   ½ cup peanut butter
2 tbsp cornstarch   1 tsp vanilla

In a saucepan on the stovetop, cook filling until thick. Transfer to a bowl and whisk in cream cheese and peanut butter. Spread over crust.

TOPPING

2 oz (60 g) bittersweet chocolate   1 tbsp icing sugar
1 cup heavy cream

Melt chocolate and let cool. Beat cream until stiff. Add icing sugar. Fold in the melted chocolate and spread over the filling.

Grilled Pineapple with Rum Sauce

½ cup butter   ¼ cup rum (coconut rum is best)
2 tbsp brown sugar   Pineapple rings

Melt butter and sugar. Add rum. Set aside. Grill pineapple until golden and grill marks form (about 2 to 3 minutes per side). Place on dessert plate; pour sauce over. Serve with whipped cream or ice cream.

Rhubarb Squares

BASE

1 cup flour
3 tbsp icing sugar
½ cup butter

Blend together and pat into 9-inch pan. Bake at 350°F for 15 to 20 minutes, until lightly browned.

FILLING

1¼ cups sugar
3 egg yolks
2 tbsp cornstarch
½ cup milk
3 cups rhubarb

Mix ingredients together and cook, stirring every minute, on high in microwave until clear and thickened. Cool. Spread over cooled crust.

TOPPING

3 egg whites
5 tbsp sugar
Pinch cream of tartar

Beat egg whites with cream of tartar until stiff. Gradually add sugar until completely dissolved (no granules can be felt when you touch the batter). Spread over filling and bake at 375°F until browned.

Butterscotch Squares

½ cup butter
1 egg
1 cup brown sugar
1 cup flour
1 cup coconut
2 tsp baking powder
2 tsp vanilla
Dash salt

Beat together butter, egg, brown sugar and flour. Add the coconut, baking powder, vanilla and salt. Bake in an 8-inch pan for 15 to 20 minutes. Cool. If desired, ice with a thin butter icing.

Flourless Chocolate Cake

7 oz (200 g) butter
7 oz (200 g) bittersweet chocolate
1 tbsp espresso powder
2 tbsp cocoa

5 eggs, separated
7 tbsp sugar
1 tsp vanilla

Preheat oven to 350°F. Place butter and chocolate in a microwave-safe bowl. Melt, until just beginning to lose shape; whisk until combined and smooth. Cool. Beat egg yolks. Sift cocoa with sugar, stir into egg yolks along with vanilla and espresso powder. Whip egg whites until stiff. Fold in half the chocolate mixture, then remainder. Pour into pan, smooth top. Bake for 25 minutes. The cake will sink while it cools. Fill with the raspberry mixture and garnish with white chocolate cream.

MELBA SAUCE

½ cup red currant jelly
2 tbsp cornstarch

2 pkgs frozen raspberries, sieved
7 tbsp sugar

Sieve raspberries, mix with sugar. Mix in red currant jelly. To ¼ cup raspberry juice, add cornstarch. Bring raspberry sugar mixture to boil. Add cornstarch and cook until thickened. Let chill until ready to use.

This is a terrific recipe for people who need to be gluten-free. It's not calorie free, however.

WHITE CHOCOLATE CREAM

6 oz white chocolate

1½ cup whipping cream

Melt chocolate with half the whipping cream. Cool. Whip remainder of cream until stiff. Fold in chocolate and continue to whip until stiff.

Turtle Cookie Bars

BASE

2 cups flour   1 cup brown sugar
½ cup butter

Mix together and pat into 9 by 13 inch pan. Bake at 350°F for 10 minutes. Arrange one cup of pecans over top.

FILLING

⅔ cup butter   1 cup chocolate chips
½ cup brown sugar

Bring butter and brown sugar to boil. Cook 3 minutes. Pour over pecans gently, being careful not to disturb the arrangement of nuts. Bake 15 to 17 minutes, until bubbling. Remove from oven, sprinkle chocolate chips over. Let stand until chocolate melts, about 5 minutes. Swirl top gently with tip of knife.

Apple Gingerbread

BASE

1 cup water   1 cup brown sugar
6 apples, peeled and sliced thin

Dissolve sugar in boiling water, add apples. Pour into bottom of 9 by 13 inch pan.

FILLING

1 cup shortening   1 tsp baking soda
⅔ cup molasses   2 tsp ginger
⅔ cup sugar   1 tsp salt
2 eggs   ½ tsp cloves
2 cups flour   ⅔ cup buttermilk or sour milk
2 tsp cinnamon

Mix dry ingredients together and set aside. Beat together shortening, molasses, sugar and eggs. Add dry ingredients alternately with buttermilk. Spoon over apples. Bake at 350°F for 45 to 50 minutes.

Peanut Butter and Bacon Blondies

2 cups brown sugar
1 cup butter, melted
2 eggs
2 tsp vanilla
2 cups flour

1 tsp baking powder
¼ tsp baking soda
Dash salt
8 slices bacon, cooked and crumbled

Line a 9 by 12 inch baking pan with parchment paper or spray with cooking spray. Preheat oven to 350°F. Cream together butter and brown sugar until light. Add eggs and vanilla. Mix together the dry ingredients. Stir to combine. Fold in the bacon. Fold batter into pan. Bake for 25 to 30 minutes. Cool completely. Remove from pan.

ICING
½ cup peanut butter
½ cup soft butter
2 to 2½ cups icing sugar
1 tsp vanilla

Milk, if needed
6 strips bacon, cooked and crumbled

Beat together peanut butter and butter. Add vanilla. Add icing sugar until consistency desired, adding a bit of milk if needed to make it spreadable. Ice squares, sprinkle with bacon. Cut when set and store in refrigerator.

Butterscotch Brickle Bars

BASE

2 cups flour ½ cup brown sugar
1 cup cold butter

Process flour, butter and brown sugar in food processor or cut in with pastry blender. Pat into 9 by 13 inch pan. Bake for 15 minutes at 350°F.

TOP

1 cup butter ⅓ cup butterscotch sundae
1 cup brown sugar   topping

Bring butter and brown sugar to a boil. Boil for 5 minutes. Add butterscotch sundae topping, pour over crust. Bake 10 minutes at 350°F.

FINAL LAYER

1 cup chocolate chips 1 cup butterscotch chips

Sprinkle chips over hot topping. Let stand 5 minutes or more. Spread evenly. Top with toasted nuts, if desired. Chill well before cutting.

Millionaire Squares

24 oatmeal cookies, crushed ½ cup melted butter

Place crumbs in 8-inch pan. Reserve a few crumbs for over top. Bake 5 minutes in 300°F oven. Cool.

FILLING

½ cup butter 1 beaten egg
2 squares semi-sweet chocolate 1 tsp vanilla
1½ cup icing sugar ½ cup nuts

Melt butter and chocolate together. Beat in icing sugar, egg, vanilla and nuts. Spread over base. Sprinkle with a few reserved crumbs. Chill well.

Salted Caramel Bars

BASE

½ cup butter
1 cup flour
⅓ cup sugar
¼ tsp salt

In a food processor, whirl dry ingredients. Add cold butter in cubes until mixture is the consistency of coarse crumbs. Pat into parchment paper-lined, 8-inch pan. Bake 20 to 25 minutes, until golden. Cool.

FILLING

½ cup butter
1 (14 oz) (414 ml) can sweetened condensed milk
¼ cup corn syrup

Microwave butter until melted. Add sweetened condensed milk and corn syrup. Microwave mixture two minutes on high, stir. Then heat one minute at a time, stirring after every minute, until it bubbles rapidly. Heat and stir every 30 seconds until it turns a deep golden color. Remember, it keeps cooking after you take it out of the microwave, so don't let it get too dark. It should take about 5 minutes, total. Pour over cooled base. Chill well.

TOPPING

12 oz (340 g) milk chocolate
1 tbsp butter

Melt together and spread over caramel. Sprinkle with sea salt. Chill and store in fridge.

Lemon Bars

BASE

1 cup flour   1/4 cup sugar
1/2 cup butter

Blend together and pat into ungreased 8-inch pan. Bake at 350°F about 20 minutes.

FILLING

1 cup sugar   Rind of 1 lemon, zested
2 tbsp flour   Juice of 1 lemon
1/2 tsp baking powder   2 eggs, beaten

Beat together and pour over hot base. Bake 25 minutes. Cool and sprinkle with icing sugar.

Butter Tart Squares

BASE

2 cups flour   1 cup butter
1/4 cup sugar   Pinch of salt

Combine and press into 9 by 13 inch pan.

FILLING

3 eggs   3/4 cup coconut (optional)
2 cups brown sugar   1 tsp vanilla
1/4 cup butter, melted   1 cup raisins
1 tbsp baking powder   3 tbsp flour
Pinch salt

Beat together, pour over crust. Bake at 350°F for 35 to 40 minutes until set but still jiggles in the centre.

Orange Zucchini Cake

½ cup raisins 　　　　　　　　1 cup boiling water

Combine in measuring cup or small bowl and set aside:

CAKE BATTER

¾ cup sugar 　　　　　　　　1 tsp baking powder
½ cup oil 　　　　　　　　　　1 tsp cinnamon
2 eggs 　　　　　　　　　　　½ tsp baking soda
½ cup bran cereal 　　　　　　¼ tsp nutmeg
2 tsp grated orange rind 　　　Pinch salt
1 tsp vanilla 　　　　　　　　1 cup shredded zucchini
1 cup flour

Combine sugar, oil and eggs. Mix well. Add bran cereal, orange zest and vanilla. Combine dry ingredients and add to egg mixture. Drain raisins well and add to batter along with zucchini. Pour into greased 7 by 11 inch pan. Bake at 325°F for 30 to 35 minutes. Ice with cream cheese icing.

CREAM CHEESE ICING

3 oz (85 g) cream cheese 　　1 to 2 tsp orange juice
1½ cup icing sugar 　　　　　1 tsp grated orange zest
1 tbsp butter

Combine icing ingredients. Frost cooled cake. Refrigerate leftovers.

When I was growing up, we lived on a farm and often had to borrow this and that from our neighbours. My brother and sister-in-law lived on the same acreage and one day Karin (my sister-in-law) returned some flour to mom. I was just beginning to get into baking all by myself and decided to make a cake. I used the flour that she had brought but couldn't figure out why a little bit of it was in a small container in with the flour. When I went to check the cake in the oven, it was bubbling all over the oven and starting to really smell. I was aghast. My sister-in-law came in and asked me what happened. When I told her, she just laughed and told me the small container was baking powder. Needless to say, I learned to question oddities.

Apple Praline Cake

2 cups flour
1 tsp baking soda
2 tsp baking powder
½ tsp salt
1 cup chopped pecans

2 eggs
1 cup sour cream or yogurt
2 tsp vanilla
1 cup sugar
1¼ cup chopped, peeled apples

Mix flour, baking soda, baking powder, salt and pecans together. Set aside. Combine eggs, sour cream, vanilla and sugar. Add other dry ingredients. Fold in apples.

Place in an 8-inch greased pan. Bake 30 minutes at 350°F. For a loaf, place in greased loaf pan and bake 50 to 55 minutes. Let rest on rack 10 minutes. Turn out onto serving plate.

PRALINE

¼ cup butter   ½ cup brown sugar

Bring to boil and cook 3 minutes. Pour over cake. Sprinkle with ½ cup chopped pecans.

Fruit Cocktail Cake

2 eggs
2 cups flour
2 tsp baking soda
1¾ cup sugar

19 oz (560 ml) can fruit cocktail, drained
2 tsp salt

Mix ingredients together, adding enough juice from fruit cocktail to moisten. Turn into a 9 by 13 inch pan. Bake at 350°F for about 1 hour.

TOPPING

1 cup brown sugar   ½ cup cream or evaporated milk
½ cup butter

Cook until sugar dissolves, about 5 minutes. Pour hot sauce over hot cake and let cool. Sometimes I like to keep half the sauce back and warm it up and serve it with the cake.

Rhubarb Pinwheels

SAUCE

1 cup rhubarb
1½ cup sugar
1 tbsp flour

½ tsp each ginger and cinnamon
1¼ cups boiling water
⅓ cup butter

Cook together until soft. Stir in butter.

FILLING

2 cups chopped rhubarb
⅛ tsp nutmeg

½ cup brown sugar
2 tbsp melted butter

PINWHEELS

2 cups flour
2 tbsp sugar
2 tsp baking powder
1 tsp baking soda

Dash salt
¼ cup cold butter
⅔ cup buttermilk

Place dry ingredients in bowl; add cold butter and cut in. Add buttermilk until dough sticks together. On a floured surface, pat out to about 9 by 12 inches. Spread filling over. Roll up and cut into 10 to 12 slices. Place in greased 9 by 13 inch pan. Pour sauce over. Bake at 350°F for 35 to 40 minutes.

A few years ago, we were in Colorado for our son's wedding. My son's favourite dessert is apple dumplings, so he'd asked that we make them for a family dinner. There were nine of us, so I said I would make it as a roll, chopping the apples and adding the other ingredients, then cutting it into pinwheels and baking it in the sauce. However, I neglected to take into consideration that we were 4,000 feet above sea level. The pinwheels turned into apple cobbler, but no one complained. With a scoop of vanilla ice cream, it was an amazing dessert. Next time, I will check on the high altitude alterations.

Rhubarb Coffee Cake with Caramel Sauce

CAKE

½ cup shortening or butter
1½ cups sugar
1 egg
2 cups flour
1 tsp baking soda
1 cup buttermilk
1½ cups chopped rhubarb

Cream together shortening and sugar. Add egg and beat well. Combine dry ingredients and add alternately with buttermilk. Fold in rhubarb. Transfer to greased 9 by 13 inch pan. Add topping.

TOPPING

½ cup brown sugar
¼ cup flour
1 tsp cinnamon
3 tbsp cold butter

Combine all topping ingredients in bowl and cut in butter until coarse crumbs form. Sprinkle over batter. Bake at 350°F for about 35 to 40 minutes. Cool 10 minutes.

CARAMEL SAUCE

½ cup butter
1 cup brown sugar
½ cup whipping cream

For the sauce, melt butter, stir in sugar; cook until dissolved. Add cream and cook 4 to 5 minutes longer until slightly thickened.

Here in Nova Scotia, we are blessed with an abundance of rhubarb. I find it's just as well to freeze it when it's available than to try to use it when it's all fresh. When you thaw it, set the frozen rhubarb in a strainer and let the liquid drain. Do not squeeze it. Letting it strain on its own gets rid of the excess liquid without losing the juiciness of the rhubarb. My favourite recipe for this spring treat is rhubarb squares. When you cook the filling, it sets up just as well with the frozen rhubarb as with fresh.

Pumpkin Pecan Dessert

28 oz (796 ml) can pumpkin
1 cup sugar
½ cup evaporated milk
4 eggs

2 tsp cinnamon
1 pkg yellow cake mix
1 cup butter, melted
1 cup chopped pecans

Line two, 9-inch pie plates or one, 9 by 13 inch pan with parchment paper. Spray with cooking spray. Combine pumpkin, sugar, milk, eggs and cinnamon. Pour into pans. Sprinkle dry cake mix over, drizzle with butter and sprinkle with pecans. Press pecans down slightly. Bake at 350°F about 1 hour or until golden. Cool 2 hours, then invert onto serving plates. Remove paper and cool completely.

SAUCE
1 cup butter
2 cups brown sugar

1 cup whipping cream

For the sauce, melt butter, add sugar and cook until sugar is dissolved. Add cream and cook 4 to 5 minutes or until slightly thickened.

Italian Dream Cake

FROSTING AND FILLING

12 oz (340 g) cream cheese, at room temperature
½ cup butter
1 tsp vanilla
1 tsp grated orange zest
4 cup icing sugar
¾ cup each shredded sweetened coconut and finely chopped toasted pecans

Combine and refrigerate until ready to use.

CAKE

2 cups all purpose flour
1½ tsp baking powder
½ tsp baking soda
1 cup butter
1¾ cup sugar
4 eggs, separated
1 tsp vanilla
1 cup buttermilk
¾ cup shredded sweetened coconut
Toasted coconut and chopped pecans for garnish

Preheat oven to 350°F. Lightly grease bottom and sides of three, 8-inch or two, 9-inch pans. Cut circles of waxed paper to fit bottom of pan. Lightly spray with non-stick cooking spray and set aside. Combine dry ingredients. Cream butter and sugar at high speed in mixer bowl until light and fluffy, about 2 minutes. Add egg yolks and vanilla. Beat until blended. Gradually add flour alternately with buttermilk, beginning and ending with flour. Stir in coconut. With clean, dry beaters, whip egg whites until peaks form. Fold gently into batter. Divide mixture evenly between pans. Bake about 25 minutes or until a toothpick comes out clean. Cool 10 minutes in pan. Run a knife around edges of cake to loosen, invert cakes onto wire racks, remove paper and cool completely. Place first layer on serving plate, spoon one third of the filling over top, spread to edges. Repeat until done. Ice top and sides of cake with remaining frosting. Sprinkle toasted coconut and chopped pecans over the cake. Refrigerate until serving.

Natural Red Velvet Cake

2 eggs
½ cup soft butter
1¼ cup granulated sugar
½ cup milk
¾ cup puréed beets
½ cup strong coffee
2 tbsp lemon juice

2 tsp vanilla
2 cups flour
⅔ cup unsweetened cocoa
2 tsp baking powder
1 tsp baking soda
Dash salt

Preheat oven to 350°F. Coat bottom and sides of a 10-inch springform pan with non-stick cooking spray and place parchment paper on bottom. Cream butter and sugar until light and fluffy. Add eggs and beat until fluffy. In another bowl, stir milk with beets, coffee, lemon juice and vanilla. In another bowl, combine dry ingredients. Using rubber spatula, combine the two mixtures, alternately. Stir only until lumps are gone. Turn into prepared pan, smooth top. Bake in centre of oven for 55 to 60 minutes, until toothpick inserted in centre comes out clean. Cool in pan on rack for 10 minutes, then remove sides and let cake cool completely. Once cool, lift onto serving plate, removing parchment paper. At serving time, either dust with icing sugar or ice with cream cheese frosting.

Coconut Key Lime Pie

1 (14 oz) (400 ml) can sweetened
    condensed milk
1 can (398 ml) unsweetened
    coconut milk
⅓ cup key lime juice

7 large egg yolks
Graham cracker crust
2 cups whipping cream
2 tbsp icing sugar
3 tbsp shredded coconut, toasted

Preheat oven to 325°F. Whisk together unsweetened coconut milk, condensed milk, lime juice and egg yolks until smooth. Pour into graham cracker crust. Bake until set but slightly jiggly in centre, about 30 minutes. Let cool on wire rack, 1½ to 2 hours. Then refrigerate 3 hours or up to a day. In a large bowl, beat cream and sugar on high until stiff peaks form. Top pie with whipped cream and sprinkle with toasted coconut.

Gingerbread Cheesecake

CRUST

1 cup finely crushed gingersnaps 2 tbsp sugar
6 tbsp butter, melted

Line outside of springform pan with heavy-duty foil. Combine crust ingredients in bowl. Press onto bottom and up 1 inch of the sides of pan. Refrigerate 30 minutes.

FILLING

4 (8 oz) (225 g) pkgs cream cheese ½ cup molasses
½ cup light brown sugar 2 tsp ground ginger
½ cup granulated sugar 1 tsp cinnamon
4 eggs ½ tsp cloves
½ cup sour cream

Heat oven to 300°F. Pulse cream cheese and sugars together in a food processor. Process 30 seconds until smooth and creamy. Add eggs, one at a time, pulsing after each addition. Add remaining ingredients. Pour into crust. Place springform pan in a larger pan, adding enough hot water to the larger pan to come halfway up the sides of the springform pan. Bake 1 hour 15 min to 1 hour 30 minutes or until edges are puffed and top is dry to the touch. Remove to rack and cool.

White Chocolate Pistachio Tart

CRUST

7 tbsp butter, melted
3 tbsp sugar
1 tsp grated lemon zest
¼ tsp salt
1 cup flour

Heat oven to 350°F. Combine butter, sugar, lemon zest and salt in a medium bowl. Add flour and stir until blended. Dough may resemble a soft oily paste. Press dough in thin layer over bottom and sides of a 9-inch tart pan with removable bottom. Make sure dough isn't too thick in corners. Bake 15 minutes. If crust is puffed, gently press down with fork. Bake an additional 5 to 10 minutes or until golden brown. Place on wire rack and reduce oven temperature to 300°F.

PISTACHIO LAYER

¾ cup unsalted pistachios
Dash of salt
½ tsp grated lemon zest
½ tsp orange zest
1 tbsp plus 1 tsp honey

Pulse pistachios and salt in food processor until nuts are finely ground. Add lemon and orange zest. Pulse to combine. Add honey. Pulse until mixture is like coarse crumbs. Carefully press mixture onto crust.

WHITE CHOCOLATE FILLING

4 oz (113 g) white chocolate, chopped
2½ tbsp boiling water
4 oz (113 g) cream cheese, softened
¼ cup sugar
1 egg
1 tbsp unsalted pistachios, chopped

Place white chocolate in a small bowl. Add boiling water. Let stand for 2 minutes, until chocolate is softened. Whisk until smooth. If the chocolate is not completely melted, microwave 15 seconds at a time until smooth. Beat cream cheese and sugar in a large bowl until smooth. Add egg and beat again. At low speed, beat in white chocolate. Pour white chocolate over pistachio mixture, spreading evenly. Bake at 300°F for 12 to 15 minutes or until filling looks set but moves slightly, like firm gelatin, when tapped. Cool completely on wire rack. Cover and refrigerate overnight. Sprinkle with 1 tablespoon pistachios before serving.

Coconut Custards

½ cup sweetened shredded coconut
1½ cups whole milk
¼ cup sugar
1 envelope unflavoured (about 10 g or 3 tsp) gelatin

1 cup "Half and Half" (coffee cream)
½ tsp vanilla
Dash salt

In a 350°F oven, toast coconut in single layer on cookie sheet about 8 minutes or until browned. Reserve 2 tablespoons of coconut for garnish. In a small saucepan, heat milk and sugar until sugar dissolves and bubbles form around the edge, about 5 minutes. Remove from heat. Stir in coconut. Cover tightly and let rest 15 minutes. Meanwhile, in a larger bowl, sprinkle gelatin over ¼ cup cold water. Let soften for 5 minutes. Strain warm coconut mixture through fine sieve into gelatin mixture, whisk until gelatin dissolves, then whisk in coffee cream, vanilla and salt. Divide among eight, 4 oz custard cups or ramekins. Refrigerate until set, about 3 hours. When ready to serve, unmold and sprinkle with reserved coconut.

Chocolate Peanut Butter Mousse Cheesecake

BASE

1½ cup chocolate wafer crumbs
¼ cup melted butter

Combine and press into bottom of greased 9-inch springform pan. Refrigerate.

MOUSSE LAYER

¾ cup creamy peanut butter
6 oz (170 g) cream cheese, softened
2 tbsp soft butter
1⅓ cup icing sugar
1¼ cup heavy cream, whipped and divided

5 oz (140 g) bittersweet chocolate, chopped
1 (3½ oz) (100 g) milk chocolate bar, chopped
⅓ cup sugar
¼ cup milk
1 tsp vanilla

Beat together peanut butter, cream cheese and butter until smooth. Add icing sugar and beat again. Fold in 1¾ cup whipped cream and spread over crust. Place bittersweet chocolate and milk chocolate in bowl. Bring sugar and milk to a boil. Pour over chocolate, whisk until smooth. Stir in vanilla. Cool to room temperature, stirring occasionally. Gently fold in remaining cream, spread over peanut butter layer and freeze 2 hours or until firm.

GANACHE

6 oz (170 g) bittersweet chocolate
⅔ cup whipping cream
1 tsp vanilla

Shaved white chocolate for garnish

Place chocolate in a bowl. Bring cream to a boil. Pour over chocolate and stir until smooth. Stir in vanilla. Cool to spreading consistency and spread over cheesecake. Refrigerate until set. Loosen cheesecake from sides of pan, remove rim. Top with shaved white chocolate.

Chocolate Pecan Pie Bars

½ cup butter at room temperature, plus 2 tbsp melted
¼ cup packed brown sugar
1¼ cup flour
½ tsp salt

3 eggs
¾ cup light corn syrup
½ cup granulated sugar
12 oz (340 g) pkg semi-sweet chocolate chips
2 cups coarsely chopped pecans

Preheat oven to 350°F. Line bottom and sides of a 9 by 13 inch pan with parchment paper or foil. In the bowl of an electric mixer, beat butter, brown sugar, flour and salt until coarse crumbs form. Pat mixture into prepared pan, press firmly onto bottom. Bake 25 to 30 minutes until lightly browned. Let cool 10 minutes. Meanwhile, in the same bowl, mix eggs, corn syrup, sugar and melted butter until combined. Add chocolate chips and pecans. Spread over crust. Bake until set, about 25 to 30 minutes. Cool completely in pan before lifting out, using foil as handles. Cut into 32 bars.

Sticky Apple Pudding with Toffee Sauce

2 cups apple cider or juice
½ cup chopped dates
4 tsp baking soda
⅓ cup soft butter
1½ cups granulated sugar
3 eggs
2 cups flour

1 tbsp baking powder
1 tsp cinnamon
½ tsp nutmeg
¼ tsp cloves
2 large tart apples, peeled, cored and diced

Put cider and dates to boil, simmering about 5 minutes until dates are soft. Remove from heat, add baking soda and let cool. Beat butter and sugar until light and fluffy. Add eggs, one at a time, beating well after each addition. Combine dry ingredients and add to butter mixture, along with date mixture. Stir in diced apples. Pour batter into greased 9 by 13 inch pan and bake in 350°F oven for 40 to 50 minutes or until toothpick inserted into centre comes out clean.

TOFFEE SAUCE
¾ cup butter
1½ cups brown sugar

¾ cup whipping cream
1 tsp vanilla

Melt butter over medium heat, add sugar and cook until sugar dissolves. Stir in cream and simmer until slightly thickened, about 5 to 8 minutes. Stir in vanilla and serve warm over warm pudding.

Crispy Peanut Butter Balls

2 cups creamy peanut butter
½ cup soft butter
3¾ cup icing sugar
3 cups crisp rice cereal or chopped peanuts

4 cups semi-sweet chocolate chips
¼ cup plus 1 tbsp shortening, divided
⅓ cup white chocolate or vanilla chips

In a large mixing bowl, beat peanut butter and butter until well combined. Gradually beat in icing sugar. Stir in cereal. Shape into 1 inch balls. Refrigerate until chilled. In a large microwave safe bowl, combine chocolate chips and ¼ cup shortening. Microwave on high, 2 minutes, then stir and continue stirring every 30 seconds until almost melted. Whisk to completely smooth. Dip balls in chocolate, then place on waxed paper-lined baking sheet. Chill again. In a microwave safe bowl, combine white chocolate chips with remaining shortening. Microwave on 70% power for 1 to 2 minutes, then whisk until smooth. Drizzle over chocolate-coated balls. Refrigerate until set.

These are always a good hostess gift. They freeze well, but if you're going to freeze them, use peanuts in place of rice krispies.

Chocolate Shortbread

2 cups butter, softened
1 cup sugar
3 ½ cups flour
½ cup cornstarch

200 g bar milk chocolate with honey almond nougat, finely chopped
Icing sugar for dusting

Heat oven to 350°F. Beat butter and sugar until light and fluffy. Combine flour with cornstarch. Gradually add to butter mixture. Stir in chocolate. Roll into 1-inch balls, place on ungreased baking sheets and press down with fingers. Bake 20 to 25 minutes. Cool on wire rack. Sprinkle with icing sugar. Makes about 5 dozen.

Rhubarb Custard Tart

1 lb (454 g) rhubarb, cut into 1-inch pieces (3½ cups)

CUSTARD
½ cup marscapone cheese (you can substitute cream cheese with a little extra cream)

SHORT CRUST PASTRY
1½ cups flour
½ tsp salt
½ cup cold butter, cubed

1 cup packed brown sugar
⅓ cup flour

½ cup whipping cream
¼ cup granulated sugar
½ tsp vanilla

3 tbsp cold water
1 tsp white vinegar

Add flour and salt to food processor, add butter, one cube at a time. Add liquid, but do not allow pastry to form a ball in the processor. Turn out and knead by hand. Roll out to fit tart pan, or chill until needed. Freeze pastry 45 minutes. Preheat oven to 400°F. Combine rhubarb, brown sugar and flour and toss to coat. Place mixture in prepared tart shell and bake about 25 minutes until rhubarb is soft. Beat together marscapone, whipping cream, sugar and vanilla. Pour marscapone mixture over rhubarb. Return to oven. Reduce heat to 350°F and bake another 25 minutes or until custard is set and rhubarb is cooked. Serve warm or at room temperature.

Something worth noting is that marscapone cheese is very expensive and sometimes, difficult to find. I have used cream cheese often for this recipe, but use slightly more cream to give it similar consistency.

Apple Dumplings

FILLING

¼ cup brown sugar
1 tsp cinnamon
¼ tsp nutmeg
2 tbsp soft butter

Mix filling ingredients together and set aside.

DUMPLINGS

2¾ cup flour
3 tsp baking powder
1 tsp salt
⅔ cup shortening
1 cup milk
4 apples, peeled and cored
(left whole)

Combine flour, baking powder and salt. Cut in shortening using pastry blender. Add milk and stir only just to moisten. Knead a few times to get a smooth dough. Pat out to ¼-inch thick (I use a sheet of waxed paper to speed cleanup). Cut into 4 squares. Place apple in centre of each square, fill cavity with filling. Wrap pastry around apple, sealing well. Use any extra pastry to decorate the top. Place in an 8-inch baking dish.

HOT SYRUP

1 cup sugar
3 tbsp butter
1 cup apple juice
1 tsp cinnamon

Bring to boil and pour around dumplings. Bake at 375°F for 40 minutes. Serve warm with ice cream or whipped cream.

Pumpkin Roulade with Ginger Butter Cream

¾ cup flour
½ tsp baking powder
½ tsp baking soda
1 tsp cinnamon
1 tsp ginger
½ tsp salt

3 large eggs, at room temperature
1 cup granulated sugar
¾ cup pumpkin purée
¼ cup icing sugar
Extra icing sugar for dusting

Preheat oven to 375°F. Grease a 13 by 18 inch baking sheet (or line with parchment paper, sprayed with cooking spray). Mix together the dry ingredients. Place the eggs and sugar in the bowl of a large mixer. Beat until pale lemon coloured. Add pumpkin, then fold in dry ingredients. Pour into prepared pan and bake 12 to 15 minutes until puffed and done. Let stand 5 minutes. Lay a dry dish towel on work surface, sprinkle ¼ cup icing sugar over and turn cake onto it. Remove paper. Roll up, using the dish towel as a guide and let stand until cool.

FILLING

1 pkg (250 g) cream cheese
4 tbsp butter

1 cup icing sugar
¼ cup minced dried ginger

Beat the filling ingredients until creamy. Unroll cake and remove towel. Spread filling over the cooled cake and roll it up again. Lay cake seam side down on serving tray, sprinkle with more icing sugar.

While my husband was still serving in the Air Force, we used to have either "international" dinners or "progressive" dinners. For the international dinners, the hosts from various countries would give us recipes to prepare and we would produce an ethnically authentic dinner. These dinners exposed us to all sorts of different dishes, increased our knowledge of other countries and enriched our experience greatly. For the progressive parties, we would involve four couples. Couple #1 would prepare the appetizer and serve it at their house. Couple #2 would do the soup or salad at their house, then the host couple #3, would do the main course. After the main course, we would all proceed to couple #4's house for dessert and coffee. Of course, the appropriate wine and coffee or tea were always served.

Swedish Raspberry Almond Bars

¾ cup butter, softened
¾ cup icing sugar
1½ cups flour
¾ cup seedless raspberry jam
3 egg whites
6 tbsp sugar
½ cup flaked coconut
6 tbsp sugar
1 cup sliced almonds, divided

In a large bowl, cream butter and icing sugar until light and fluffy. Gradually add flour and mix well. Press onto bottom of sprayed 9 by 13 inch pan. Bake at 350°F for 18 to 20 minutes or until lightly browned. Spread jam over crust. Beat egg whites until stiff. Gradually beat in sugar, 1 tablespoon at a time, until stiff peaks form. Fold in coconut and ½ cup of almonds. Spread over jam. Sprinkle with remaining almonds. Bake at 350°F for 18 to 22 minutes, until golden brown. Sprinkle with icing sugar before serving.

Shortbread Tarts with Fruit and Cheese Filling

TARTS

1 cup butter
½ cup icing sugar
1½ cup flour
1 tbsp cornstarch

Mix tart ingredients together and pat mixture into mini-muffin tins using fingers to distribute the dough at even thickness. Prick bottom with a fork. Bake 20 minutes at 300°F. Prick bottoms again and let cool. (This can be prepared days ahead and frozen).

FILLING

8 oz (225 g) cream cheese, softened
1 (14 oz) (414) can sweetened condensed milk
⅓ cup lemon or lime juice
1 tsp vanilla

Beat all filling ingredients together and refrigerate until ready to serve. Just before serving, spoon into tart shells and garnish with fresh fruit.

Strawberry Rhubarb Cream Dessert

BASE

2 cups flour	1 cup butter, melted
1 cup chopped pecans	¼ cup sugar

Combine base ingredients and press into greased 9 by 13 inch pan. Bake at 350°F for 18 to 20 minutes until golden brown. Cool on wire rack.

FILLING

1 cup brown sugar	1 pkg (250 g) cream cheese, softened
3 tbsp cornstarch	
5 cups chopped fresh or frozen rhubarb (thawed)	1 cup icing sugar
	1¼ cups heavy whipping cream, divided
1 cup sliced strawberries	

Combine brown sugar and cornstarch. Add rhubarb and toss until well combined. Bring to a boil over medium heat, stirring often, (I cook it in the microwave) until thickened. Remove from heat. Cool. Add the strawberries. In a large bowl, combine cream cheese and icing sugar until smooth. Fold in 1 cup whipped cream. Spread over crust. Top with rhubarb mixture, then remaining whipped cream. Refrigerate 3 to 4 hours, until well chilled, before serving. Garnish with a sprinkle of brown sugar.

Banana Roll

6 large eggs
3½ tsp baking powder
⅓ tsp salt
1 cup granulated sugar
1 cup cake flour
1½ tsp vanilla
3 very ripe bananas, mashed well or puréed

Break up the 3 bananas until no lumps remain. Let stand a few minutes to darken. Break eggs into large beater bowl, add baking powder and salt and beat on high speed until very foamy. Gradually beat in sugar with beater set on high. Continue beating until mixture triples in size and holds its shape when dropped from beater. Add vanilla. Fold in ⅓ of the flour with ⅓ of the bananas and continue until well blended. Turn onto waxed paper or parchment paper-lined, 11 by 15 inch baking pan. Bake at 400°F for about 25 minutes in centre of oven, until the top springs back when touched. Carefully loosen edges and turn cake out onto generously icing sugared-dish towel. Let rest 5 minutes. Roll up including towel. Place on rack to cool completely.

FILLING AND FROSTING

1 pkg (250 g) cream cheese
½ cup soft butter
1 egg yolk
½ medium banana, mashed (optional)
3 cups icing sugar

Beat cream cheese and butter until well blended. Add egg yolk and banana, if using. Combine with icing sugar until of spreading consistency. Using about half of the filling, unroll the cake and fill with cream cheese mixture. Roll up tightly and place on serving platter. Ice with remainder of cream cheese mixture, using bar-like strokes. Chill at least 2 hours before serving.

When I was a kid, we lived on a small farm, about 20 acres. My dad had to supplement our income by working in a sawmill in the neighbouring town. Every morning during berry season my brother and I were booted out of bed at 6:30 to pick strawberries or raspberries (whichever was in season) so dad could take them with him and sell them in town. This made for a good work ethic: out to pick berries, then breakfast, then school.

Crème Brûlé

This recipe is probably my all time favorite dessert. This recipe was from a cruise ship and I have never found another one quite as good.

2 cups cream
1 tsp pure vanilla extract
6 tbsp granulated sugar
4 large egg yolks
4 tbsp sifted brown sugar

In a large saucepan, combine cream, vanilla and sugar. Heat until almost boiling (small bubbles will form around sides of pan). Whisk the egg yolk and add about 1 tablespoon of the hot mixture, whisking all the time, continue to do so until both mixtures are incorporated. Remove from heat and pour into four flame-proof ramekins that have been arranged in a 9-inch pan. Fill pan with very hot water so it comes about halfway up the sides of the ramekins. Cover lightly with foil and bake on centre rack of a 300°F oven for about 40 to 50 min, until they appear set but are still slightly shaky in the centre. Remove from water and chill at least 3 hours. When ready to serve, sprinkle each with 1 tablespoon of sifted brown sugar and place under the broiler until the sugar melts. (I use a small butane torch). You can serve this immediately with the caramelized sugar or chill it and then break the caramel crust to get to the custard. I also like to put fresh raspberries on the side for garnish.

The first year we had high-grade appliances for the show, we had a wall oven. It was not self-cleaning. I explained to the guys who worked there that I didn't clean my oven at home and as a volunteer, I sure wasn't doing it on the set. I told them repeatedly that it had to be cleaned. One day during taping, the floor director suddenly made the slashing sign, meaning "Stop, stop!" As I turned to ask why, I glanced behind me: the oven looked like an indoor fireplace! Debris inside it was ablaze. Guess who cleaned the oven that night (not me).

Apple Strudel

¼ cup raisins
1 tbsp bourbon or apple cider
4 cups diced peeled apples
⅓ cup plus 1 tbsp sugar, divided
¼ cup toasted pecans
1 tsp ground cinnamon
1 tsp grated lemon zest
Dash salt
¼ cup dry breadcrumbs
½ tsp ground cardamom
8 sheets phyllo dough, thawed
5 tbsp melted butter
1 tbsp turbinado sugar or raw sugar

Heat oven to 400°F. Line a cookie sheet with parchment paper. Combine raisins and bourbon and microwave 45 seconds. Let stand 30 minutes. Combine apples, raisins, ⅓ cup sugar, pecans, cinnamon, lemon peel and salt in large bowl. Combine breadcrumbs, remaining 1 tablespoon of sugar and cardamom in small bowl. Unroll phyllo, cover with a damp cloth. Place 1 sheet phyllo on work surface, brush with melted butter and crumb mixture, repeat, layering remaining phyllo, melted butter and crumb mixture. Spoon apple mixture down centre, leaving a 2-inch border. Fold in sides of phyllo, roll up apple mixture. Place seam side down on baking sheet. Brush with remaining butter and sprinkle with turbinado sugar. Bake 25 to 30 minutes, or until golden brown and apples are tender. Cool on wire rack for 30 minutes. Serve warm or cold. Good with sweetened whipped cream.

I love phyllo pastry but it can be difficult to work with. You buy it frozen, then let it thaw in the refrigerator. That step is important, if you thaw it at room temperature, it gets gooey on the outside. When you unwrap the sheets, make sure they are covered with a damp cloth. If you are only using a few sheets, rewrap the rest, tightly, using the paper included. Seal it with a piece of tape, place it back in the box and refreeze it. This can't be done more than twice, as the dough dries out. When you start working with the thawed sheets, instead of brushing them with melted butter, spray them with butter-flavored cooking spray. The spray gives the same crispy texture without all the calories. Keep any unused sheets covered with a damp towel. Proceed by laying out one sheet at a time on the work surface, spraying it, adding the filling, then repeating until your recipe is complete.

Macadamia Lemon Bars

1 cup flour
¼ cup icing sugar

½ cup butter, melted
¼ cup chopped macadamia nuts

FILLING

1 cup sugar
2 tbsp flour
½ tsp baking powder
¼ tsp salt
2 eggs

2 tbsp lemon juice
2 tsp lemon zest
2 tbsp chopped macadamia nuts
Icing sugar for garnish

Preheat oven to 350°F. Mix flour, sugar and melted butter until crumbly. Stir in nuts. Press onto bottom and ½ inch up sides of a sprayed or parchment paper-lined, 8-inch baking pan. Bake 15 minutes or until lightly browned. Meanwhile in a small bowl, whisk together sugar, flour, baking powder and salt. Beat in eggs, lemon juice and lemon zest until blended. Pour over hot crust. Sprinkle with remaining nuts. Bake 10 to 15 minutes or until lightly browned. Cool completely on wire rack. Cut into bars. Sprinkle with icing sugar.

Grasshopper Pie

2 cups crushed chocolate wafer crumbs

2 tbsp sugar
½ cup butter, melted

Mix together and press onto bottom of buttered 9-inch springform pan, saving some for garnish. Set aside.

FILLING

8 oz (226 g) jar marshmallow cream
¼ cup crème de menthe

2 cups whipping cream, stiffly beaten

Beat together until smooth. Fold in whipped cream. Tint a nice light green with vegetable coloring. Chill or freeze until ready to serve.

Banana Split Dessert

CRUST

2 cups graham wafer crumbs
½ cup butter, melted
¼ cup brown sugar

Combine crust ingredients and pat into bottom of 8-inch pan. Chill.

FILLING

2 cups icing sugar
2 eggs
½ cup butter
1 tsp vanilla
1 can (398 ml) crushed pineapple
2 to 3 bananas
2 cups whipping cream
2 tbsp sugar
1 tsp vanilla
Maraschino cherries for garnish

Beat butter, icing sugar and eggs together until creamy. Add vanilla. Spread over crust.

Drain crushed pineapple and pour over filling. Slice bananas over the top.

Whip cream with sugar and vanilla until stiff. Put over bananas. Chill. Garnish with maraschino cherries. This recipe is best if you let it stand overnight in the fridge to develop the flavours. Also can be frozen. Make sure you thaw it 24 hours in the refrigerator before attempting to slice it.

Apple Kuchen

½ cup butter
1 pkg yellow cake mix
½ cup flaked coconut (optional)
2½ cups sliced, peeled apples or
   1 can (796 ml) apple pie filling
½ cup sugar (omit if using canned pie filling)
1 tsp cinnamon
1½ cups sour cream
2 egg yolks

Mix butter, cake mix and coconut (if using) until crumbly. Pack into ungreased, 9 by 13 inch pan. Bake 10 minutes at 350°F. Arrange apple slices over warm crust. Mix sugar and cinnamon and sprinkle over the apples. Mix sour cream and egg yolks and drizzle over apples. Bake 25 minutes or until edges are brown. Do not overbake.

White Chocolate Mousse with Raspberry Sauce

6 oz (170 g) white chocolate
½ cup milk, warmed
1 envelope (approx. 3 tsp) unflavoured gelatin
1 tsp vanilla
2 egg whites
1 cup whipping cream
1 tsp lemon juice

Melt chocolate with ¼ cup milk. Whisk until smooth, set aside. Sprinkle gelatin over remaining milk and warm until gelatin dissolves (30 seconds in microwave). Add to chocolate with vanilla. Mix until smooth. Cool. Beat egg whites until stiff, fold into chocolate. Whip cream, fold in with lemon juice. Pour into serving dishes and chill until firm.

RASPBERRY SAUCE

15 oz (425 g) pkg frozen raspberries, with juice
Juice of ½ a lemon
½ cup sugar
2 tsp cornstarch
¼ cup raspberry liqueur (optional)

Combine berries and lemon juice in blender. Purée. Strain to remove seeds. Pour mixture into small saucepan, add sugar, bring to a boil. Simmer 15 minutes. Mix cornstarch with liqueur (or water) and add. Cook 1 minute, or until thickened and clear. Cool.

Brandied Peaches

28 oz (796 ml) can peach slices, drained, reserving 2 tbsp syrup
4 tbsp butter
½ cup brown sugar
½ tsp cinnamon
¼ cup brandy

Drain peaches and place in a shallow baking dish. Combine syrup and everything but brandy and pour over the peaches. Bake 20 to 22 minutes until hot at 325°F, stirring occasionally. Add brandy and serve with ice cream.

Blueberry Layer Dessert

CRUST

21 "Digestive" cookies, crushed to fine crumbs	¼ tsp cinnamon
	½ cup melted butter
1 tsp sugar	

Mix together crust ingredients and pat into 9 by 12 inch pan. Bake 12 minutes at 350°F. Cool.

FILLING

8 oz (226 g) cream cheese	2 eggs
½ cup sugar	1 tsp vanilla

Combine filling ingredients and spread over crust. Bake 20 minutes.

3 cups frozen or fresh blueberries	½ cup cold water
½ cup water	3 tbsp sugar
1 tbsp lemon juice	3 cookies, crushed
4 tsp cornstarch	

Combine berries, water, sugar and lemon juice in saucepan. Bring to a boil. Dissolve cornstarch in cold water, add and cook until thickened. Pour over baked layer. Cool.

1 cup whipping cream	1 tsp vanilla.
2 tbsp sugar	

Whip cream, sugar and vanilla. Spread over blueberry layer. Garnish with crumbs. If making ahead, do not put the crumbs on until serving time.

Apple Crêpes with Buttered Rum Sauce

CRÊPES

3 large eggs
1 cup flour
1 cup milk
1 tbsp sugar
½ cup water
½ tsp salt
2 tbsp melted butter

Blend together and let stand 30 minutes. Heat 8-inch skillet, brush with butter and cook ¼ cup batter at a time to make crêpes.

FILLING

2 lb apples (about 6 medium)
2 tbsp butter
½ cup brown sugar
¼ tsp cinnamon
¼ cup pecans, finely chopped

Melt butter in a pan. Add brown sugar, cinnamon and apples. Cook until soft (about 4 minutes in microwave). Add pecans. Place ¼ cup filling on each crêpe. Roll up. Place in a buttered dish. When ready to use, reheat 5 minutes if fresh, 20 minutes if in fridge. Meanwhile make sauce and caramel.

SAUCE

¾ cup brown sugar
1 tbsp cornstarch
1 cup water
½ cup butter
⅓ cup dark rum

Combine all ingredients, for sauce, except rum. Bring to a boil and simmer 5 minutes. Remove from heat. Add rum.

CARAMEL (OPTIONAL)

In a heavy saucepan, melt ½ cup granulated sugar, stirring constantly until it turns golden. Remove from pan immediately.

Strawberry Yogurt Panna Cotta

2 cups sliced fresh or frozen berries (either strawberries or raspberries)
½ cup sugar
1 cup no fat yogurt
4 tsp unflavoured gelatin
¾ cup 5% cream
1 tsp vanilla

Purée berries, sugar and yogurt. Strain to remove seeds. Sprinkle gelatin over ¼ cup cream to soften. Heat remaining cream to boil, stir in gelatin until dissolved. Add vanilla. Whisk into berry mixture. Pour into six 6-ounce ramekins or moulds. Refrigerate at least 4 hours.

1 ½ cup sliced berries
2 tbsp sugar
1 tbsp balsamic vinegar

Combine the sliced berries, sugar and balsamic vinegar. Unmold panna cotta onto serving plate. Garnish with the berry/balsamic mixture.

Date Squares

1 cup flour
1 cup butter
½ tsp baking soda
1 cup brown sugar
Dash salt
2 cups rolled oats

Mix dry ingredients, cut in butter until the consistency of coarse crumbs. Pat half into a buttered 8-inch pan.

FILLING

½ lb (225 g) dates, finely chopped
2 tbsp brown sugar
½ cup water or orange juice

Cook filling ingredients until thick (about 3 to 4 minutes in microwave). Add 1 teaspoon of vanilla. Pour over base and sprinkle remaining crumbs over. Bake at 350°F for 30 to 40 minutes until golden brown.

Layered Pumpkin Mousse

5 egg yolks
1 cup sugar
3½ cups whipping cream
2 cups pumpkin purée
2 tsp vanilla
1½ tsp cinnamon
½ tsp ginger
¼ tsp nutmeg
Salt
3 tbsp dark rum
1 tsp unflavoured gelatin
3 oz shredded dark chocolate

Whisk together egg yolk, ¾ cup cream and ¾ cup sugar. Cook until thickened. Transfer to a metal bowl and set in a bowl of ice. When cool, add pumpkin, spices and vanilla and salt. Stir 1 tablespoon of rum with gelatin, until softened, then heat second amount of rum until hot (30 seconds in microwave). Add heated rum to cold rum to dissolve gelatin. Whisk into pumpkin mixture. Chill until cold. Beat remaining cream with 2 tablespoons of sugar until stiff. Add 1 tablespoon of rum. Layer in large trifle bowl or individual serving dishes, ending with whipped cream. Garnish with shredded dark chocolate.

Apple Cream Lasagne

9 oven ready lasagne noodles
1 can (796 ml) apple pie filling
6 tbsp brown sugar
½ cup chopped pecans
1 pkg cream cheese
1 egg
1 tsp vanilla
1 cup whipping cream
¼ cup butter
½ cup soft bread crumbs
¼ cup white sugar

Soak noodles in warm water. Mash apple pie filling. Stir in 3 tablespoons of brown sugar, pecans and cinnamon. Set aside. Beat cream cheese with egg, brown sugar and vanilla. Whip cream. Fold into cheese mixture. Melt butter, stir in bread crumbs and sugar. Drain noodles. In a shallow pan that has been sprayed with non-stick cooking spray, spread ½ the apple mixture over bottom, cover with 3 noodles. Spread noodles with apple mixture. Spread with ½ the cream cheese mixture. Cover with 3 noodles and spread with half the apples, 3 noodles and remaining cream. Sprinkle crumbs directly over cream. Bake at 350°F for 30 to 40 minutes. Let stand 20 minutes before serving. Top with vanilla ice cream.

German Chocolate Cake

1 Swiss chocolate cake mix, made according to package directions, cooled.
⅓ cup brown sugar
½ cup evaporated milk or cream
2 egg yolks
⅓ cup shortening
1 tsp vanilla
1¼ cups flaked coconut
1 cup chopped pecans

Combine sugar, milk, egg yolks and shortening. Cook, stirring constantly, over medium heat until mixture comes to a full boil. Remove from heat. Stir in vanilla, coconut and pecans. Cool 15 minutes, then spread between layers and on top of the cake. Can also be made in a 9 by 13 inch pan.

Sticky Toffee Pudding with Toffee Sauce

12 oz (340 g) pkg pitted dates, chopped
2½ cups water
1½ cups granulated sugar
½ cup butter, softened
1½ tsp finely grated lemon rind
½ tsp salt
4 eggs
1½ tsp vanilla
2¾ cups flour
2 tsp baking soda

Bring dates and water to a boil. Cook until dates are soft. Add baking soda. Let cool and smash with potato masher. Beat together butter, sugar, lemon rind and salt. Beat in eggs. Beat in vanilla. Whisk together dry ingredients and add to butter mixture alternately with dates. Scrape into a 10-inch Bundt pan that has been greased and floured. Bake 55 to 60 minutes in 350°F oven until toothpick inserted in centre comes out clean. Let cool on rack 15 minutes. Invert cake onto plate.

TOFFEE SAUCE
¾ cup butter
1 cup brown sugar
¾ cup whipping cream
2 tbsp lemon juice
Pinch salt
2 tbsp brandy

Melt butter and whisk in sugar until dissolved. Cook, whisking, until caramel colored, about 5 minutes. Averting face, whisk in cream, lemon juice and salt and bring back to boil. Cook until thickened, about 5 minutes. Whisk in brandy. Pour about ¾ cup over warm cake. Let stand to absorb.

To serve:
Drizzle each serving with warmed remaining sauce.

Chocolate Coma Cookies

1 cup slivered almonds, toasted
4 oz (113 g) bittersweet chocolate
1 cup dried cherries
12 oz (340 g) pkg semi-sweet chocolate chips
2 cups oatmeal
2 cups flour
1 tsp baking powder
1 tsp baking soda
½ tsp salt
1 cup soft butter
1 cup brown sugar
1 cup white sugar
2 eggs
1½ tsp vanilla

Toast almonds and cool. Chop bittersweet chocolate into tiny pieces. Combine cherries and chocolate chips. Set aside. Sift together dry ingredients. Beat butter until creamy and add sugars and eggs. Combine with vanilla and then add dry ingredients. Add chocolate, chocolate chips and almonds. Spoon out by tablespoons onto parchment-lined baking sheets. Bake at 350°F for 12 to 14 minutes. I have made this recipe using dried cranberries for the cherries, also using white chocolate chips for the bittersweet chocolate. Do not be afraid to vary the ingredients to suit your family's tastes.

Apricot Whip

1 (3 oz) (85 g) pkg orange jello
1 cup boiling water
1 can (398 ml) apricots, drained
1 cup apricot syrup
1 cup whipping cream

Put jello and boiling water in blender. Add apricots. Cover and run at high until gelatin is dissolved. Remove inner cap and add apricot juice. Pour into a metal dish and refrigerate until almost firm. Whip cream and fold into apricot mixture. Chill until serving.

Nanaimo Maple Mousse Cake

CAKE

48 fudge covered graham wafer cookies
1 cup unsweetened flaked coconut
½ cup finely chopped walnuts
½ cup butter, at room temperature
1 egg
¼ cup sugar
1 tsp vanilla

In a food processor, pulse 25 cookies until finely ground. Transfer to a large bowl. Stir in coconut and walnuts. Beat together butter, egg, sugar and vanilla. Set bowl over simmering water and cook, stirring constantly, until thickened, about 5 minutes. Pour over crumb mixture and stir to combine. Evenly press onto bottom of 8-inch springform pan that has been sprayed with non-stick cooking spray. Cover and refrigerate.

FILLING

1 pkg (3 tsp) unflavoured gelatin
¼ cup warm water
1 cup pure maple syrup
2 cups heavy cream
¼ cup hot fudge sundae topping, at room temperature
1 tbsp icing sugar

In a two-cup bowl, sprinkle gelatin over warm water and stir to dissolve. Heat maple syrup over medium heat until very warm, about 2 minutes. Slowly stir in gelatin mixture until well combined. Cool in fridge 15 to 20 minutes or over a bowl of ice water. Beat 1½ cup of cream until stiff peaks form. Fold into cooled maple mixture. Spread over crust. Cover and refrigerate 1 hour or until set. Stir 1 tablespoon of water into fudge topping. Spread over top of mousse. Cover and refrigerate 30 minutes. Beat remaining cream with icing sugar until peaks form. Remove sides of springform pan. Press remaining graham crackers onto sides of cake before serving. Top with whipped cream and drizzle with a little fudge topping.

Mocha Hazelnut Trifle with Hazelnut Brittle

BRITTLE

1 cup sugar
½ cup water
¼ cup chopped hazelnuts
2 tbsp grated orange zest
½ tsp baking soda

Combine sugar and water in microwave-safe measuring cup. Cook until mixture boils and darkens, about 5 minutes. Watch carefully as it can go from golden to burnt in a few seconds. Stir in hazelnuts and zest. Add baking soda and stir until foaming stops. Pour onto parchment paper-lined baking sheet, spread in a thin layer. Cool and break into bits.

FILLING

2 cups whipping cream
1 cup icing sugar
¼ cup coffee liqueur
¼ cup butter
8 oz (226 g) milk chocolate, chopped
1 cup marscapone cheese, at room temperature
1 cup coffee
6 large soft lady fingers or pound cake

Divide whipping cream in half. Beat 1 cup with icing sugar until soft peaks form. Beat second cup to firm peaks. Beat in liqueur. Refrigerate both until ready to use. Place marscapone in large bowl, beat until smooth. Melt chocolate and beat into cheese mixture until smooth. Fold in cream whipped with sugar. Reserve. Bring coffee to boil and boil until reduced to ½ cup – about 8 to 10 minutes. Set aside. Chop enough of the brittle to yield one cup. Stir brittle into chocolate mousse. Place a thin layer of the liqueur cream onto bottom of trifle dish. Crumble half the lady fingers over cream, then drizzle with half the reduced coffee. Repeat, ending with mousse. Garnish with remaining liqueur whipped cream and hazelnut brittle.

Frozen Peanut Butter Pie

If you wish, you can use a ready-made chocolate crumb crust.

CRUST

1 cup semi-sweet chocolate chips
⅓ cup butter
2½ cups rice crisp cereal

Carefully mix together and press into the pie shell. Chill 30 minutes.

FILLING

8 oz (225 g) cream cheese, at room temperature
1 (14 oz) (414 ml) can sweetened condensed milk
¾ cup peanut butter
2 tbsp lemon juice
1 tsp vanilla
1 cup whipping cream, whipped

Beat cheese until smooth. Add milk and peanut butter. Stir in lemon juice and vanilla. Fold in whipped cream. Pour into crust, drizzle with melted chocolate. Freeze 4 hours or more.

Frozen Daiquiri Soufflé

This recipe makes enough for 16 servings but can easily be halved. It also keeps well in the freezer.

8 eggs, separated
Dash salt
2 cups sugar
2 tbsp (2 envelopes) unflavoured gelatin
½ cup lemon juice
½ cup lime juice
½ cup rum
2 cups whipping cream
Grated zest of 2 lemons
Grated zest of 2 limes
Green food coloring

Blend lime juice, lemon juice and grated zests. Beat egg yolks until pale lemon coloured. Add juice mixture and 1 cup sugar. Soak gelatin in rum and set aside to bloom. Cook egg yolk mixture over low heat until custard mixture coats a spoon. Add gelatin to custard until gelatin dissolves. Tint a nice light green and set aside in the fridge until almost set. Beat egg whites until foamy. Add remaining 1 cup sugar gradually and beat until stiff. Whip cream until stiff. Fold egg whites into custard, then whipped cream. Pour into large serving dish or individual serving dishes and freeze.

Chocolate Raspberry Mousse Cake

CRUST

1½ cups chocolate crumbs
6 tbsp melted butter

¼ cup seedless raspberry jam (or warm regular jam slightly and pass through a fine sieve)

Heat oven to 350°F. Stir cookie crumbs and butter together. Press onto bottom of a 9-inch springform pan. Bake 10 minutes. Cool. Brush raspberry jam over crust.

FILLING

8 oz (225 g) semi-sweet chocolate   1½ cups cream

Heat cream to boiling, pour over chocolate. Stir until melted. Cool until cold but still liquid. Whip until stiff peaks form. Pour into crust. Chill 1 hour.

FILLING

1 cup cream
¼ cup raspberry jam, sieved

¼ cup icing sugar

Whip until stiff, pour over filling.

TOPPING

¾ cup whipping cream

6 oz (170 g) semisweet chocolate, chopped.

Melt together, cool 30 minutes. Pour over cake and chill until set.

Sweet Marie Bars

½ cup brown sugar
½ cup peanut butter

½ cup corn syrup

Combine in saucepan on stove top; melt, but do not let boil. Add:

2 cups rice crisp cereal
½ cup chopped peanuts

1 tbsp butter

Pat into greased 8-inch pan. Let cool until firm. Frost with chocolate frosting.

Cherry Nut Bars

1 cup brown sugar
½ cup butter
½ cup milk
1 cup coconut
1 cup chopped nuts
8 maraschino cherries, chopped
1 cup graham wafer crumbs
18 whole graham wafers

Combine sugar, butter and milk in a small saucepan. Bring to a boil. Remove from heat, add crumbs, nuts, coconut and chopped cherries. Arrange 9 graham wafers in bottom of 8-inch pan. Top with crumb mixture, then top with 9 whole graham wafers. Press graham wafers down slightly. Chill.

ICING

2 tbsp soft butter
1 cup icing sugar
1 tbsp milk (or cherry juice)
½ tsp vanilla

Blend together and frost squares. Chill well. Sprinkle with a few graham wafer crumbs.

Cranberry Zucchini Cake

20 oz (591 ml) can pineapple chunks
1 cup vegetable oil
3 cups flour
1¾ cup sugar
2 tsp vanilla
1 tsp baking powder
1 cup grated zucchini
1 tsp baking soda
1 cup chopped cranberries
1 tsp salt
½ cup chopped pecans
3 eggs
Icing sugar

Drain pineapple, reserving ½ cup juice. Place pineapple and reserved juice in a blender or a food processor and purée. Combine dry ingredients in a large bowl. In a smaller bowl, beat together, eggs, oil, vanilla and pineapple mixture. Stir into dry ingredients. Fold in zucchini, cranberries and nuts. Pour into greased and floured tube pan or 9-inch springform pan. Bake at 350°F for 55 to 65 minutes or until toothpick inserted in centre comes out clean. Cool 10 minutes on rack. Remove from pan and cool completely. Dust with icing sugar.

Fresh Apple Cake

This recipe is from my son's mother-in-law, who has an abundance of apples in her yard. Best served warm. Excellent for breakfast

4 cups diced apples   1 cup sugar

Blend together and let stand 10 minutes.

½ cup vegetable oil   2 tsp cinnamon
1 cup sugar   1 cup nuts
2 cups flour   2 eggs
1 tsp salt   2 tsp vanilla
1 tsp baking soda

Stir together sugar, oil, nuts and vanilla. Add dry ingredients, then fold in apples. Pour into greased and floured 9 by 13 inch pan. Bake at 350°F for 45 to 50 minutes.

Carrot Cake

2 cups white sugar
1⅓ cups vegetable oil
1 tsp vanilla
4 eggs
3 cups finely grated carrots
1 cup raisins
1 cup chopped nuts

2 tsp baking soda
1 (8 oz) (226 g) pkg glazed cherries, chopped
1 tsp salt
2 tsp baking powder
3 cups flour
1 tsp cinnamon

Beat sugar, oil, vanilla and eggs until fluffy. Mix dry ingredients and add to egg mixture. Fold in carrots, raisins, nuts and cherries. Pour into a 9 by 13 inch pan that has been lined with parchment paper or foil. Bake at 350·F about 50 to 60 minutes until toothpick inserted in centre comes out clean.

CREAM CHEESE FROSTING

1 (250 g) package cream cheese
½ cup soft butter
3 to 4 cups icing sugar

1 tsp vanilla
Enough milk or cream to achieve spreading consistency

Beat cream cheese and butter together until well combined. Add icing sugar and vanilla and then add enough milk to achieve spreading consistency.

I did a tradeshow some years ago and was introduced to a famous Maritime chef. We shared information about our backgrounds and cooking philosophy. He strongly believed that "In order to prepare good food, one has to know what good food tastes like." I've always maintained that belief. In today's age of busy working families, too many young people reach adulthood not knowing what food prepared from scratch tastes like. It's amazing how they react when they're given "real" homemade food, not something out of the supermarket's freezer section.

Chocolate Cheesecake Cupcakes

FILLING

8 oz (226 g) cream cheese
⅓ cup sugar
1 egg
1 cup chocolate chips

Cream above ingredients together and set aside.

BASE

1½ cups flour
½ tsp salt
1 cup sugar
1 cup water
⅓ cup oil
¼ cup cocoa
1 tsp vinegar
1 tsp baking soda
1 tsp vanilla

Combine and fill greased muffin cups one third full. Drop a spoonful of the filling on top. Bake at 350°F for 20 to 25 minutes until chocolate part springs back when touched.

Texas Sheet Cake

2 cups sugar
2 cups flour
1 cup butter
1 cup water
4 tbsp cocoa
½ cup buttermilk
2 eggs, beaten
1 tsp baking soda
1 tsp vanilla

In a large saucepan, bring butter, water and cocoa to a boil. Place flour and sugar in a large bowl. Pour the boiling mixture over and add buttermilk, eggs, soda and vanilla. Pour into 10 by 15 inch cookie sheet with sides. Bake at 400°F for about 20 minutes. Meanwhile, make icing.

ICING

½ cup butter
4 tbsp cocoa
6 tbsp milk
3 cups icing sugar
1 tsp vanilla
1 cup chopped pecans

Bring butter, cocoa and milk to boiling. Add icing sugar, vanilla and pecans. Pour hot icing over hot cake and let stand until cool.

Butter Tarts

2 eggs, beaten
2 cups brown sugar
2 tbsp vinegar
1 tsp vanilla
⅓ cup melted butter
1½ cup raisins
24 pre-made tart shells

Beat all ingredients except raisins. Put raisins into tart shells, dividing evenly. Pour filling into shells. Place on cookie sheet and bake 10 minutes at 425°F, then reduce heat to 325°F for an additional 20 to 25 minutes, depending on how runny you like the filling.

Nanaimo Bars

BASE

½ cup butter
¼ cup white sugar
5 tbsp cocoa
1 tsp vanilla

Cook above ingredients over double boiler until thick. Add:

1 cup coconut
½ cup chopped walnuts
2 cups graham wafer crumbs

Pat into sprayed 9-inch pan. Set aside.

FILLING

¼ cup butter
2 tbsp custard powder (or vanilla instant pudding)
2 cups icing sugar
3 tbsp milk

Cream together and spread over base. Chill well.

TOPPING

3 squares semi-sweet chocolate, melted
1 tbsp butter

Melt together and spread over filling. Chill well. Keep in refrigerator.

Sugar Crusted Ginger Cookies

¾ cup soft butter
¾ cup brown sugar
1 oz (28 g) pkg 4-serving butterscotch instant pudding
1 egg
2 cups flour
1 tsp baking soda
1 tbsp ground ginger
1½ tsp cinnamon
½ cup finely chopped crystallized ginger
Additional ¼ cup sugar for rolling

Mix together butter and brown sugar until creamy. Add egg and pudding mix. Fold in remaining ingredients. Divide into 2 rolls. Wrap in plastic wrap. Chill at least 1 hour. Heat oven to 350°F. Unwrap roll, roll in sugar and slice into ½-inch slices. Place on parchment paper-lined cookie sheets. Bake 11 to 13 minutes. Cool 5 minutes. Remove to rack to cool completely.

Layered Lemon Squares

BASE
2 cups flour
1 cup butter
1 cup chopped pecans

Mix until crumbly. Press into 9 by 13 inch pan. Bake 10 to 15 minutes at 400°F until slightly golden. Cool.

FILLING
2 (8 oz) (226 g) pkgs cream cheese
1 cup icing sugar
1 cup whipping cream, whipped

Beat together cheese and sugar. Fold in cream. Spread on cooled crust.

SECOND FILLING
425 g pkg lemon pie filling, prepared as directed.

Cool. Pour over cheese layer.

TOPPING
2 cups whipping cream
2 tbsp sugar
1 tsp vanilla

Beat cream until stiff. Add sugar and vanilla. Pour over other layers. Decorate with pecans, if desired.

HOLIDAY RECIPES

These are a few of my family favorites that I do every Christmas, as well as my mother-in-law's Gumdrop cake and Christmas pudding.

164

Christmas Pudding

This is a long-standing traditional Christmas treat from my mother-in-law's kitchen.

1 cup suet
1 cup molasses
1 cup sour milk
2½ cups flour
1 tsp cinnamon
½ tsp nutmeg
¼ tsp cloves
1 tsp baking soda
3 cups dried fruit (dates, cherries, raisins, walnuts, pecans, candied pineapple or whatever is available)

Take half a cup of the flour and toss it with the fruit. Mix the remaining ingredients and add the fruit. Put into a pudding basin (I use a stainless steel bowl, well buttered). Cover with double thickness of buttered foil. Place in steamer and steam for about 3 hours. If it's still soft, bake for 30 minutes in a 300° F oven.

I usually make this 3 to 4 weeks before Christmas. Soak some cheesecloth in brandy or rum and wrap it around the pudding. Tightly wrap in foil and then reheat before serving.

HARD SAUCE

½ cup soft butter
1½ cup granulated sugar
2 tbsp rum or brandy
1 egg white, stiffly beaten

Cream the butter and sugar. Add brandy. Fold in stiffly beaten egg white. Cover and refrigerate several hours to set up. Then, using a spoon, scrape thin slices off of the hard sauce and place the slices on the hot pudding.

Fruitcake Bars

⅓ cup butter
12 oz (340 g) box vanilla wafers, crushed
1 cup pecan halves
¾ cup chopped dates
¾ cup red cherries, halved
¾ cup green cherries, halved
½ cup glazed pineapple
1 (14 oz) (414 ml) can sweetened condensed milk
¼ cup bourbon or rum or milk

Melt butter in 10 by 15 inch pan. Sprinkle with crushed wafers. Arrange fruit and nuts over crumbs. Combine milk and bourbon. Pour evenly over fruit. Bake at 350°F for about 30 minutes. Cool. Cut into small squares while still flexible.

Sticky Toffee Shortbread Bars

BASE

1 cup flour
¼ cup sugar
½ cup cold butter, cubed

Pulse together in food processor until coarse crumbs form. Pat into parchment paper-lined 8-inch pan. Bake at 350°F for 25 minutes.

FILLING

½ cup finely chopped dates
¾ tsp baking soda
4 tsp flour
½ tsp baking powder
Dash salt
2 eggs
½ cup sugar
⅔ cup corn syrup
3 tbsp butter, melted
2 tsp vanilla
1 cup chopped pecans

Stir dates with ¼ cup water and bring to boil. Simmer about 3 minutes, until dates are soft. Add soda and set aside to cool. Mix flour, baking powder and salt. Whisk together eggs, sugar, corn syrup, melted butter and vanilla. Stir in flour mixture. Fold in dates and pecans. Pour over hot crust and bake at 350·F until filling is set and deep golden brown (30 to 35 minutes). Cool completely. Cut into squares. Dust with icing sugar, if desired.

Stained Glass Cookies

1 cup soft butter
¾ cup brown sugar
1 tsp vanilla
Dash salt

2½ cups flour
1 cup slivered almonds
½ cup each red and green cherries

Cream together butter and sugar; add vanilla, salt and flour. Add almonds and cherries. Knead until smooth and dough forms an even ball. Form into rolls. Wrap in plastic wrap and chill until firm (or freeze dough to be thawed and baked later). When ready to bake, heat oven to 350°F. Slice cookies and bake.

Brown Sugar Shortbread

1 lb (454 g) butter
1 cup brown sugar

4 cups flour

Cream butter and sugar. Work in flour by hand. Knead until it becomes smooth and clings together. At this point, if you want to make shapes, chill well before rolling. If you're in a hurry, roll into small balls, flatten with the bottom of a glass using a piece of waxed paper to prevent sticking, add a small bit of cherry and bake at 300°F for about 20 to 25 minutes

Pecan Sandies

1 cup butter
⅓ cup sugar
2 tsp vanilla

2 tsp water
2 cups flour
1 cup finely chopped pecans

Cream together butter, sugar, vanilla and water. Add flour, then finely chopped pecans. When the dough forms a firm ball and all clings together, shape into 1-inch balls. Bake on ungreased cookie sheets 20 minutes in 300°F oven. Cool 10 minutes, then roll in icing sugar. Make sure your cookies are still warm or the sugar won't stick.

Chocolate Hazelnut Butter Crisps

2¼ cups flour
¼ tsp salt
1¼ cups butter, softened
1¼ cups icing sugar
2 tsp vanilla

2 tsp instant coffee dissolved in 2 tsp hot water
1 cup toasted hazelnuts, finely chopped
Semi-sweet chocolate, melted

Stir together flour and salt. Cream butter. Gradually add in sugar, vanilla and coffee. Slowly add in dry ingredients until smoothly combined. Stir in nuts. Form dough into 1-inch balls and place on greased cookie sheets. Flatten each cookie to about 2-inch thickness using the bottom of a glass dipped in flour or using a small piece of waxed paper. Bake at 325°F for about 10 to 12 minutes, until lightly browned. Cool. Dip edges in melted chocolate and sprinkle with more hazelnuts, if desired.

Jelly Cookies

½ cup butter
½ cup sugar
1 egg
2 tbsp milk

1½ cups flour
2 tsp baking powder
1 tsp vanilla

Cream together butter, sugar, egg, milk and vanilla. Add dry ingredients and form into small balls. Place on cookie sheet and press a dent in top of each cookie with your thumb. Fill with jelly. Bake 15 to 20 minutes at 325°F.

Gum Drop Cake

This is my mother-in-law's recipe that's been in her family for generations. Absolutely wonderful at Christmas time.

1 cup butter
2 cups white sugar
3 eggs
1 cup warm milk
1 tsp vanilla
1 tsp lemon flavouring
1 lb (454 g) gumdrops (the sugar coated kind; remove any black ones)
3½ cups flour
1½ tsp baking powder

Cream together butter and brown sugar. Add eggs, milk and flavourings. Save ½ cup flour to coat gumdrops (it keeps them from sticking together). Add remaining flour and baking powder. Fold in gumdrops. Pour into greased and floured 10-inch bundt or angel food cake pan. Bake about 1½ hours at 325°F.

Mock Pound Cake

This was a recipe my mother used for years, in place of the traditional Christmas cake. It makes a lot and of course, with a big family, usually feeds them all.

2 cups butter	2 cups raisins
2 cups sugar	2 cups cherries, halved
¾ cup boiling water	6 eggs
¾ cup milk	1 tsp nutmeg
6 cups flour	4 tsp baking powder

Cream together butter and sugar and beat until light and fluffy. Add boiling water until blended, then add milk. Stir 2 cups flour into batter. Add eggs, then 2 more cups flour. In a separate bowl, mix remaining 2 cups flour with nutmeg and baking powder, then fold in cherries and raisins. Add to batter. Spread into greased loaf pans and bake 1 to 1½ hours at 350°F. Makes four 9-inch loaves.

Cranberry and White Chocolate Shortbread

1¾ cups flour	¾ cup icing sugar
½ cup cornstarch	1 tsp vanilla
½ tsp salt	½ cup dried cranberries
1 cup soft butter	½ cup white chocolate chips

Preheat oven to 325°F. Line a 9 by 13 inch pan with parchment. Beat together butter and sugar, then vanilla. Combine dry ingredients. Stir into butter mixture, then add cranberries and chocolate. Using floured hands, pat mixture into pan. Prick all over with fork. Bake at 325°F for 40 to 50 minutes or until edges are golden. Remove and let stand on a wire rack 30 minutes Using paper, lift out of pan and cut into 1 by 2 inch bars. Dust with icing sugar, if desired.

Sugar Cookies

1½ cups flour
⅓ cup sugar
1½ tsp baking powder
1 egg yolk

3 tbsp milk
½ cup soft butter
½ tsp vanilla

Cream butter. Add sugar gradually, beating well between additions. Add egg yolk and mix well. Add dry ingredients alternately with milk. Chill dough thoroughly. Roll out ¼-inch thick on a lightly floured board. Cut with Christmas cookie cutters and bake on parchment-lined baking sheet, 5 to 8 minutes at 375°F. Cool on rack and ice with butter icing.

Tosca Cake

SPONGE CAKE
½ cup butter
½ cup sugar
Grated rind of 1 lemon

2 eggs
½ cup flour
½ tsp baking powder

Cream together butter, sugar and lemon rind until fluffy. Add eggs, beating well. Stir in dry ingredients. Bake in sprayed or parchment paper-lined 8-inch pan at 325°F for 20 to 25 minutes, until top springs back when touched.

TOPPING
⅓ cup butter
¾ cup sliced almonds
⅓ cup sugar

1 tbsp flour
2 tsp milk

Melt butter; stir in remaining ingredients. Bring to a boil. Spread evenly over cake and bake 10 to 15 minutes until lightly browned.

Rich Hot Fudge Sauce

1 cup whipping cream
¾ cup butter
1½ cups brown sugar
⅓ cup white sugar
Pinch salt

1 cup cocoa
½ cup corn syrup
2 squares unsweetened chocolate, chopped
3 tsp vanilla

Combine cream and cubed butter. Cook until butter melts. Add sugars and salt. Cook until dissolved. Add cocoa and corn syrup. Cook until blended. Add chocolate and cook until melted. Reduce heat to low and simmer 10 to 15 minutes, until thickened. Cool. Store in fridge. Reheat in microwave.

Graham Cracker Fruit Cake

2 cups dark seedless raisins
2 cups golden raisins
1 cup pitted dates, chopped
½ cup halved candied cherries
⅔ cup slivered candied pineapple
⅓ cup diced candied orange peel
¼ cup diced candied citron (or use 1¾ cups bulk mixed fruit in place of last 4 ingredients)

1 cup chopped nuts
2 cups port wine
1 tbsp vanilla
1 cup soft butter
1 cup sugar
6 eggs
5 cups graham wafer crumbs

In a large bowl, mix fruit, nuts, 1 cup port and vanilla. Cover tightly and let stand overnight or up to 3 days. In a large mixer bowl, at medium speed, beat butter and sugar until creamy. Beat in eggs, 2 at a time, until blended. Alternately beat in graham wafer crumbs and fruit mixture, ¼ at a time, including any excess wine in fruit mixture, until thoroughly combined. Grease 1 tube pan or two, 9 by 5 inch loaf pans and line with foil. Pour in batter. Bake 3 to 3½ hours at 325°F or until toothpick inserted in centre comes out clean. Cool in pan on rack. Remove foil. Store at least 2 weeks, sprinkling daily with the remainder of the port.

Peanut Butter Fudge

1 cup butter, melted
12 oz (1½ cups) peanut butter
1 cup cocoa
1 lb (454 g) icing sugar
1 tsp vanilla

Mix cocoa and sugar. Melt butter, add peanut butter to combine, then add to cocoa mixture with vanilla. Pack mixture into greased 8-inch pan. Cut into squares while still warm.

Christmas Cake

¼ lb (113 g) candied pineapple, slivered
1 lb (454 g) pitted dates, chopped
½ lb (225 g) mixed peel
½ lb (225 g) candied cherries
½ lb (225 g) whole almonds
¼ lb (113 g) chopped walnuts
2 lb (905 g) sultana raisins
1 lb (454 g) Lexia raisins
1 lb (454 g) currants
5 cups flour
1 tsp baking soda
1 lb (454 g) butter
1½ cups brown sugar
1½ cups white sugar
12 eggs
1 tsp vanilla
Juice and rind of 1 lemon
¼ tsp nutmeg
2 tsp cinnamon
1 tsp mace
2 tsp cream of tartar
Rum or brandy

Mix all fruit together and coat with 1 cup flour. Cream together butter and sugars, then add eggs, 2 at a time along with vanilla, lemon juice and lemon rind. Combine remaining flour with the spices and add to butter mixture. Fold in fruit. Line four, 9 by 5 inch loaf pans with parchment paper, spray well with non-stick cooking spray. Spoon batter into pans. Bake in 325°F oven for 1½ to 2 hours, until toothpick inserted in centre comes out clean. If possible, put a pan of water in the oven along with the cakes so the steam will cook the cake and keep it moist. Cool on rack, then peel off parchment. Drizzle with rum or brandy and tightly wrap in foil and store 2 weeks or more, until ripened.

Snowballs

2 eggs, beaten
1 cup white sugar
2 tbsp butter
1½ cups finely chopped dates
2 cups rice crisp cereal
Coconut

In a saucepan, melt butter. Beat eggs and sugar together. Add to butter along with dates. Stirring constantly, cook until mixture forms a paste, about 7 or 8 minutes. Mix in cereal. Let cool until you can handle it without burning your hands. Butter your hands, roll mixture into balls, roll balls in coconut. Cool completely.

Cheese Shortbread

1 tub (approx. 8 oz/226 g) sharp old cheese spread
½ cup butter, softened
2¼ cups flour
Apple jelly for filling

Work all ingredients together until cracks form in the dough. Chill well. Roll out thinly and cut into 2-inch circles. Put a dab of apple jelly in centre and fold over, sealing well. Bake at 300°F for 10 to 15 minutes.

Cherry Loaf

1 cup butter
1¾ cup white sugar
3 eggs
¾ cup milk
1½ cup chopped maraschino cherries
3 cups flour
2 tsp baking powder
2 tsp vanilla
1 tsp lemon extract

Cream butter and sugar, add eggs and milk. Dust the cherries with ½ cup flour, add remaining dry ingredients with extracts and fold in cherries. Bake at 350°F for about 1 hour. Makes 1 long loaf or two, 9 by 5 inch loaves.

Chocolate Peanut Butter

1½ cups peanut butter
½ cup chocolate chips, melted
¼ cup soft butter
¼ cup icing sugar

1 tsp vanilla
1 tsp instant coffee dissolved in
   1 tbsp hot water

Mix first five ingredients; stir until smooth. Combine coffee and water and stir into first mixture. Place in decorative jar and serve.

Microwave Peanut Brittle

1 cup sugar
½ cup corn syrup
1 cup salted peanuts

1 tsp baking soda
1 tsp vanilla
1 tbsp butter

Mix sugar and corn syrup. Microwave on high 4 to 5 minutes until completely dissolved. Add peanuts and cook on high 3 to 4 minutes more until golden – do not let it get too dark as it continues to cook after you remove it from the oven. Add vanilla and butter, then baking soda. Stir until it stops frothing. Pour out onto a sprayed foil-lined baking sheet and cool. Break into pieces when cold. Make sure you test your microwave first. The first batch I made with a new microwave came out like a lump of charcoal. Check it after 3 minutes and then proceed. Make sure you have on long oven mitts when tipping the mixture out onto the cookie sheets, as it burns your skin really quickly.

When we lived in Moose Jaw, SK, no one had ever heard the name McElman. Every time I phoned someone, I'd have to say "It's McElman" and spell it out. My daughter could spell it out by the time she was four years old. One day when I was expecting our son, my neighbour and I were discussing baby names. Since the baby was due at Christmas, I said we'd been considering "Heather Noelle" as a name if the baby was a girl. My daughter, looking very confused said, "but mommy, there's no 'L' in Heather."